Introduction

This book is intended for children to be taught about the basic rules that exist at school and why they matter. Following school rules are extremely important so they can be safe, stay focused, and maintain discipline. They play an essential role in ensuring children know how to behave and produce responsible students. Additionally, they promote effective teaching and learning.

We suggest using this book in the first month of school, however, it is not only for the beginning of school but to remind students about school and classroom rules for all holiday breaks. These rules can be read aloud to the children in classrooms, and it includes activities that help reinforce them in class or at home to improve social skills. Additionally, parents can use this book for their children to help them understand and acquire social skills.

We try to focus on the positive way to teach rules and not the negative outcome of not following them. The Rules are divided into 3 areas: Classroom Rules, Recess Rules, and General Health Rules, after the "Rules" section of the book, we include activities that will help the children to understand them and another section to color them. At the end of the book, you'll find a medal as a reward that can be cut out and given to children and a contract that can create a sense of responsibility that can reflect on their behavior, which will help them to improve skills like self-monitoring and self-control.

RULES

IN THE CLASSROOM

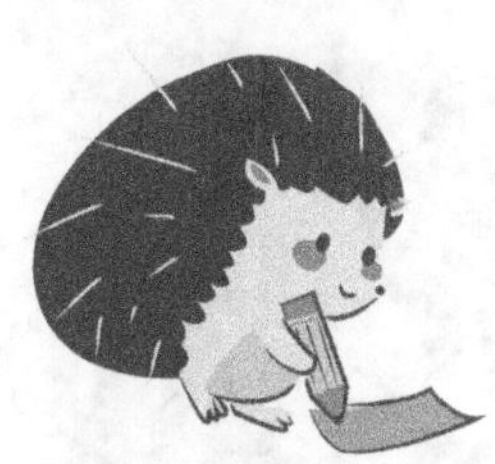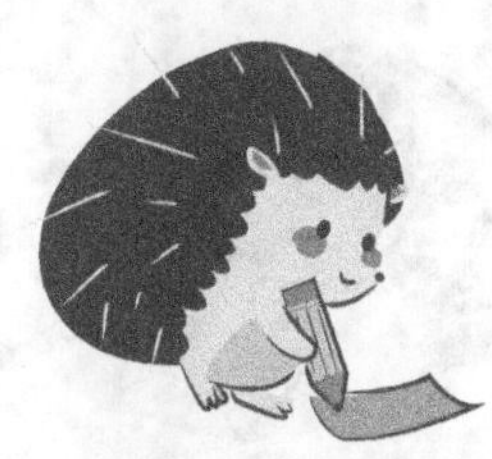

1. LISTEN TO THE SPEAKER

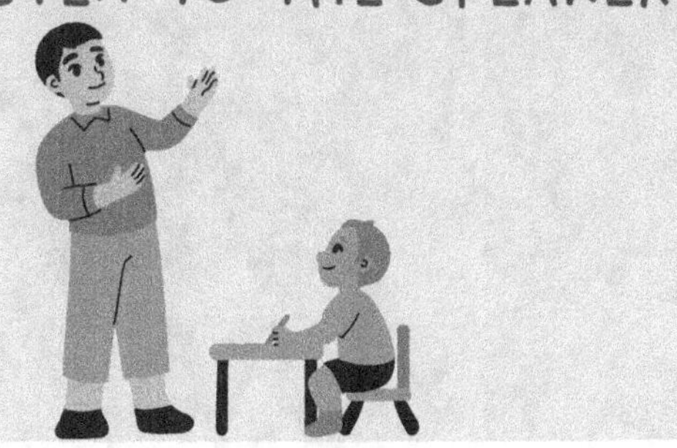

2. RAISE YOUR HAND TO SPEAK

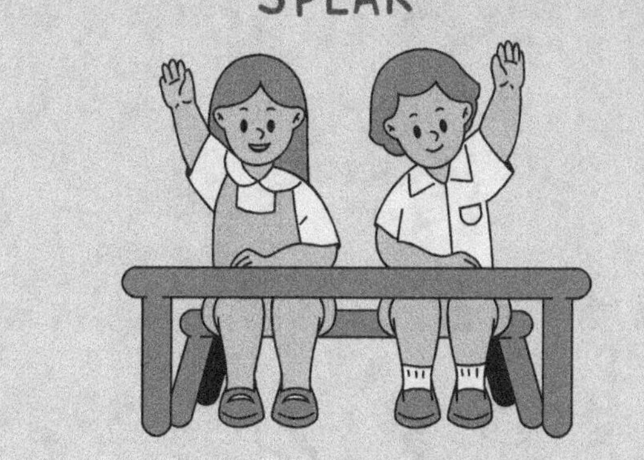

3. RESPECT YOUR CLASSMATES AND TEACHER

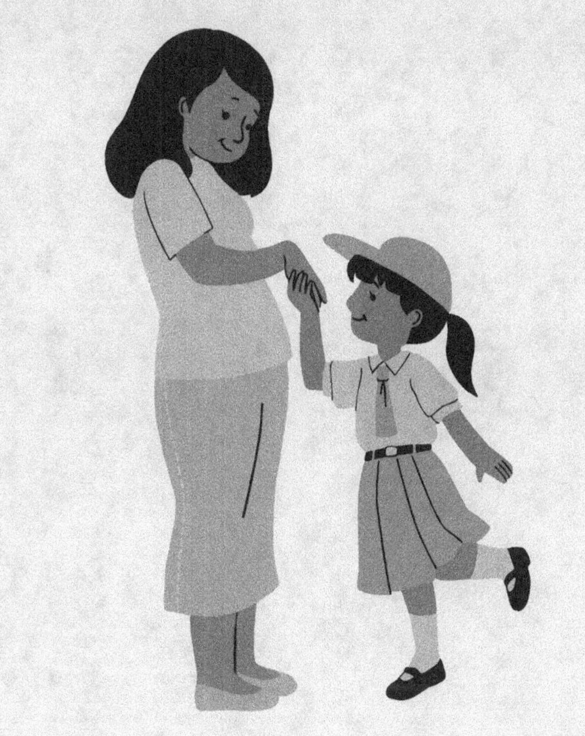

4. KEEP YOUR HANDS TO YOURSELF

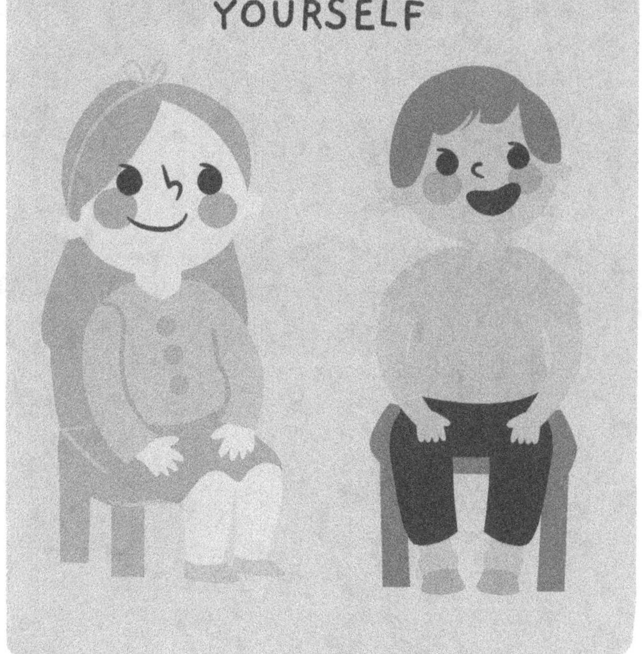

5. SAY PLEASE AND THANK YOU

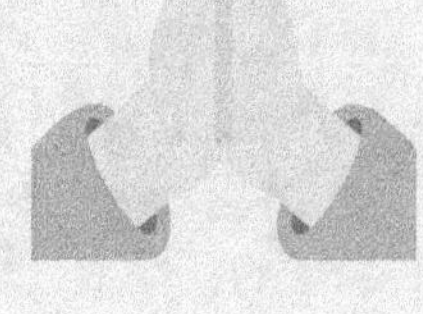

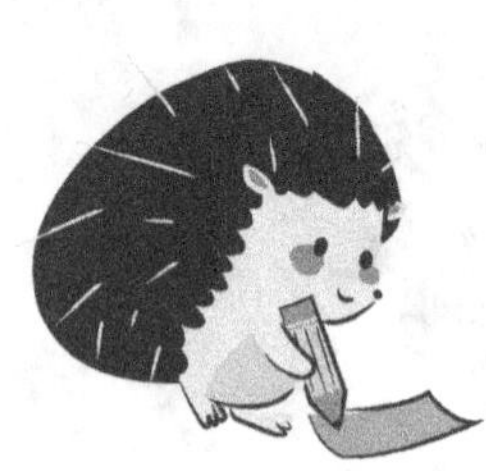 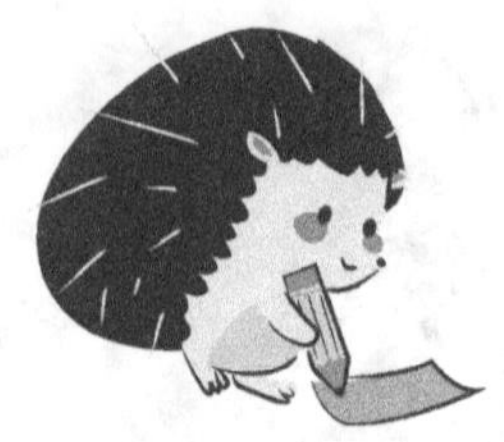

IN THE CLASSROOM

6. FOLLOW DIRECTIONS

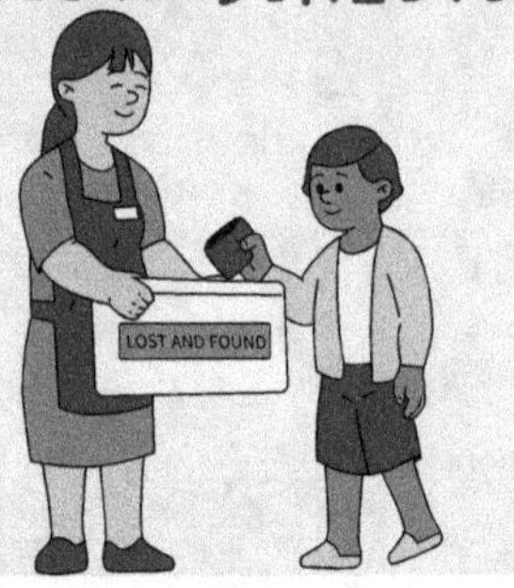

7. WE SPEAK SOFTLY IN CLASS

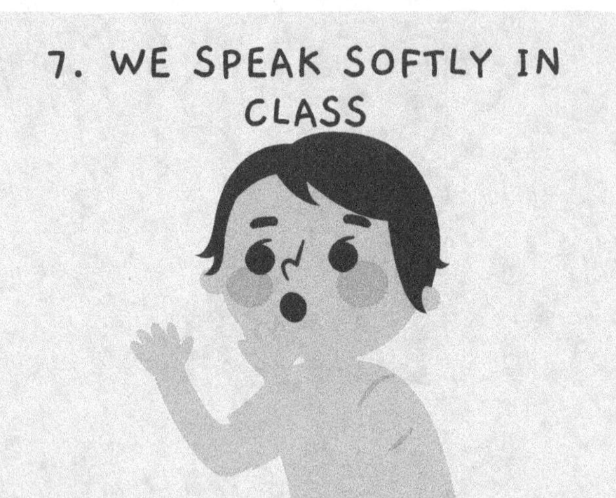

8. HELP EACH OTHER

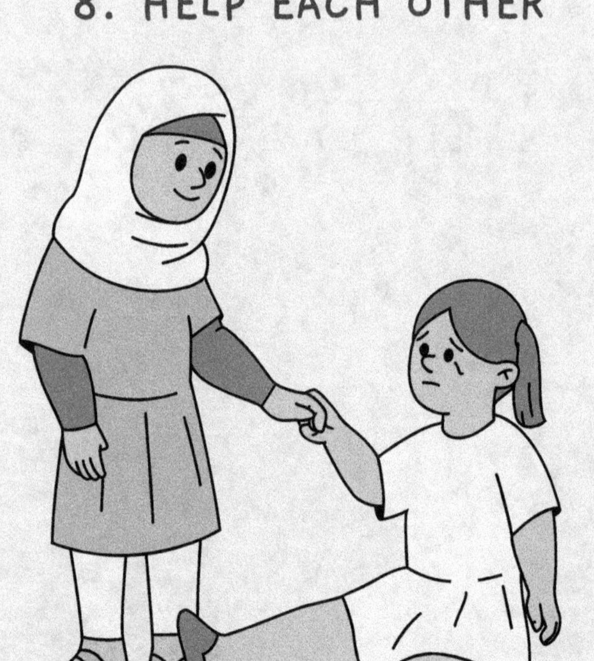

9. WE DON'T CHEAT

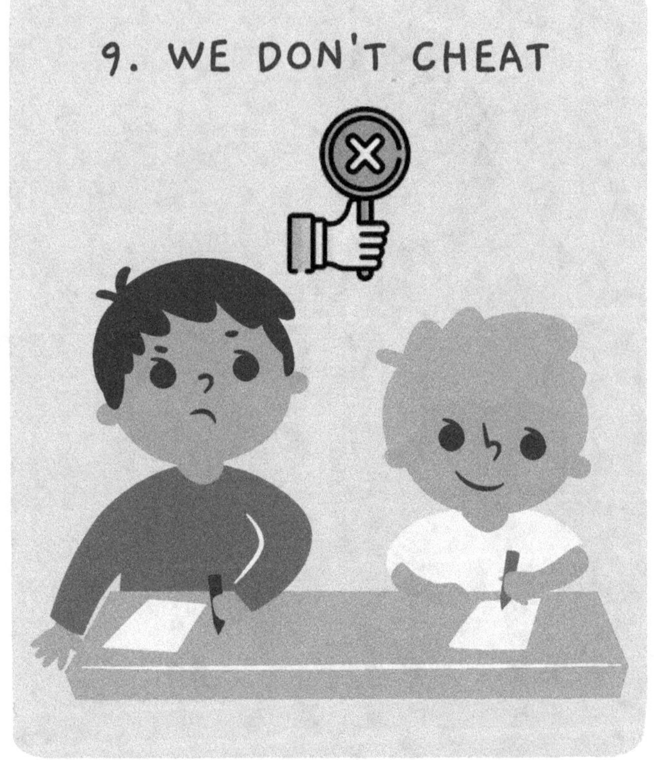

10. USE KIND WORDS

 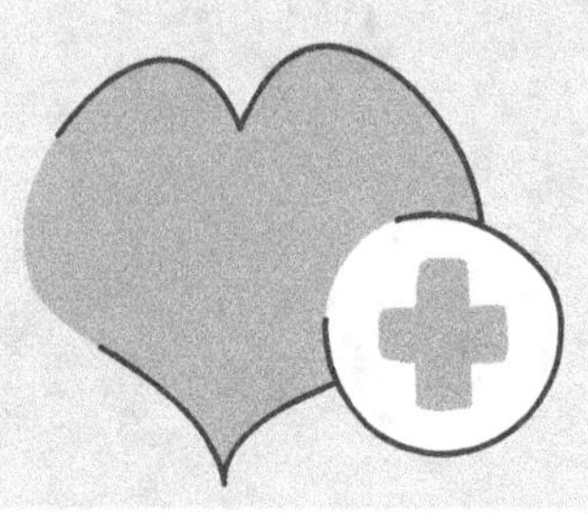 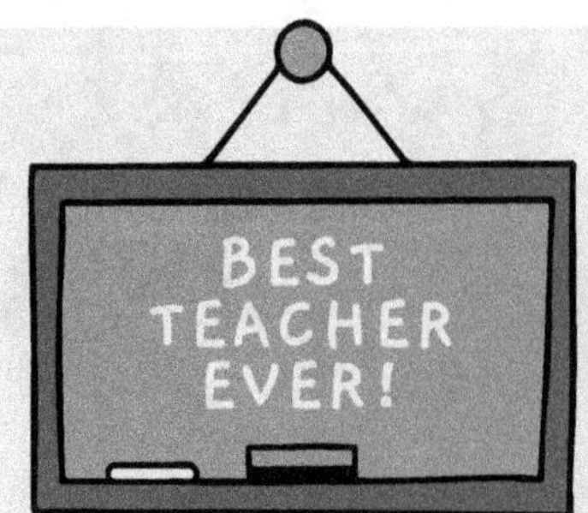

IN THE CLASSROOM

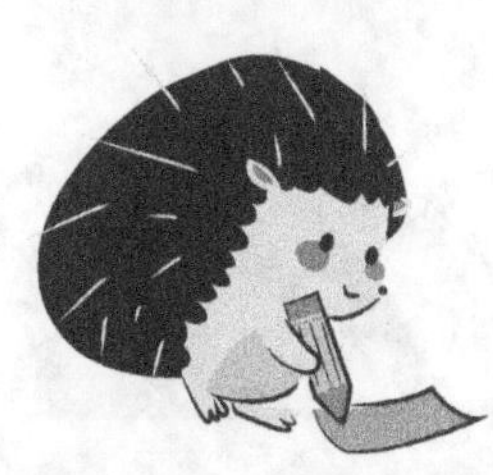
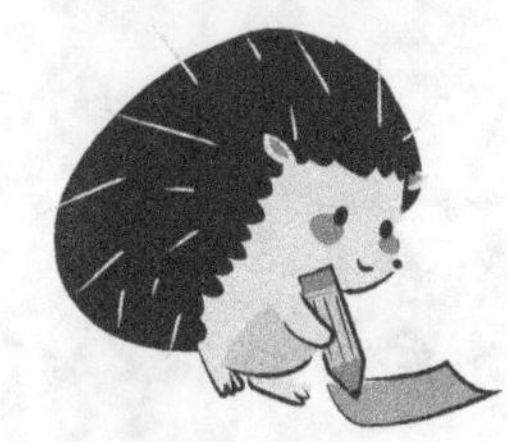

11. RESPECT OTHERS' PROPERTY

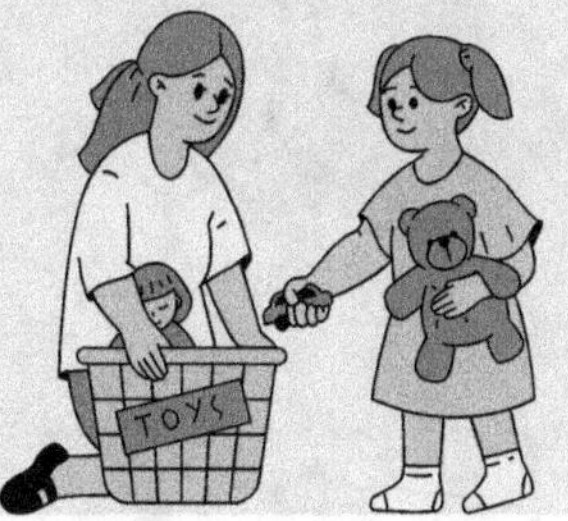

12. ALWAYS ASK FOR HELP IF YOU NEED IT

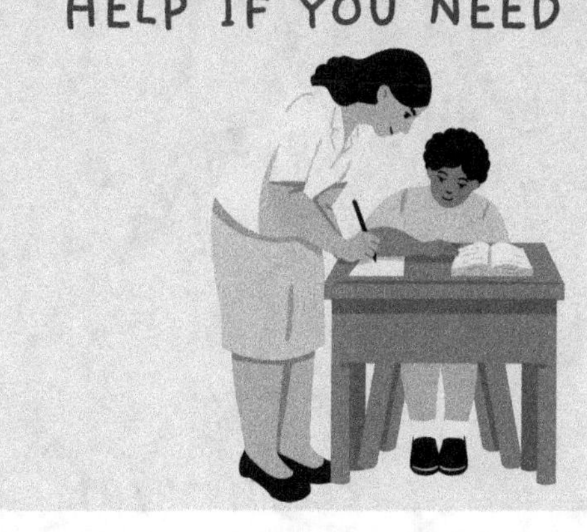

13. USE TECHNOLOGY APPROPRIATELY

14. IF YOU MAKE A MESS, CLEAN IT UP

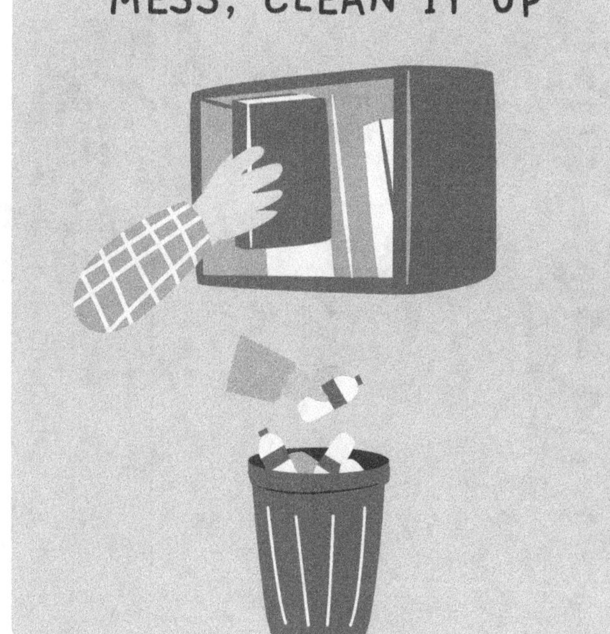

15. IF YOU SEE SOMEONE IN DANGER, TELL AN ADULT

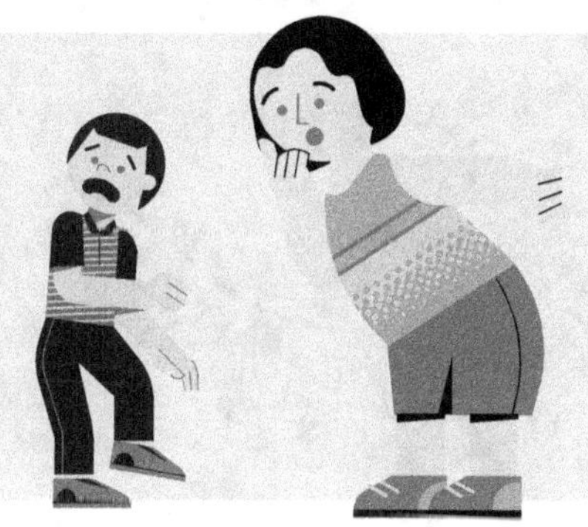

IN RECESS:

16. BE SAFE ON THE PLAYGROUND
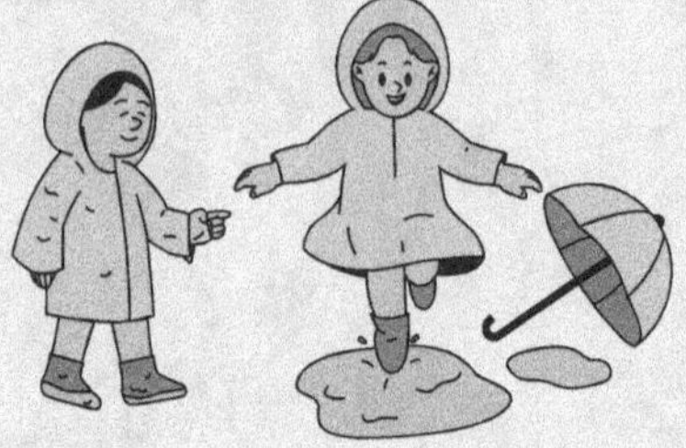

17. PLAY FAIR
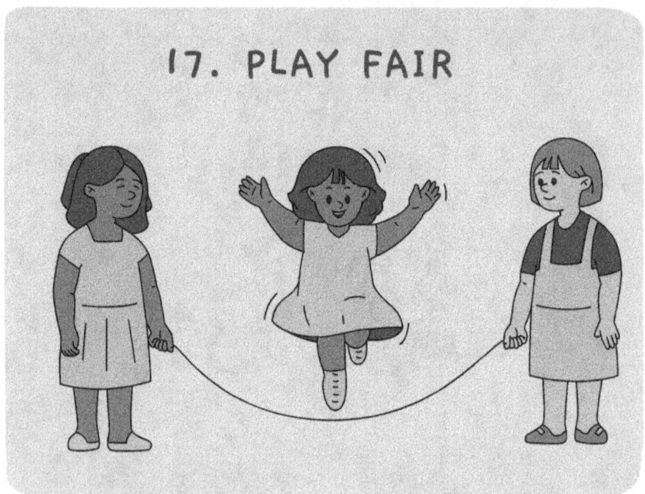

18. WAIT YOUR TURN
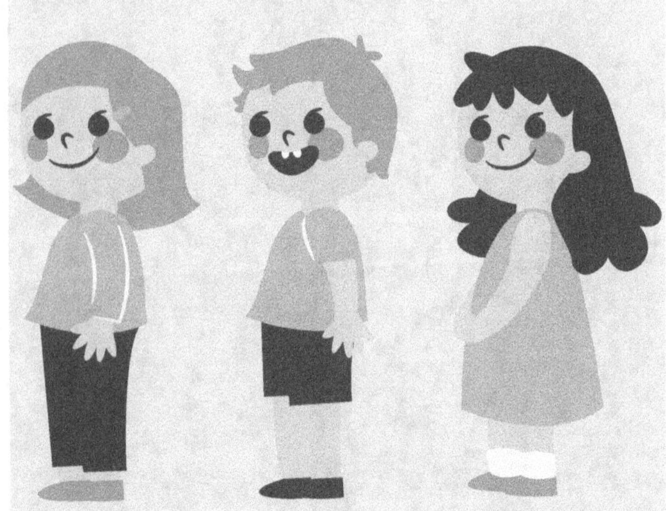

19. SHARE WITH OTHERS
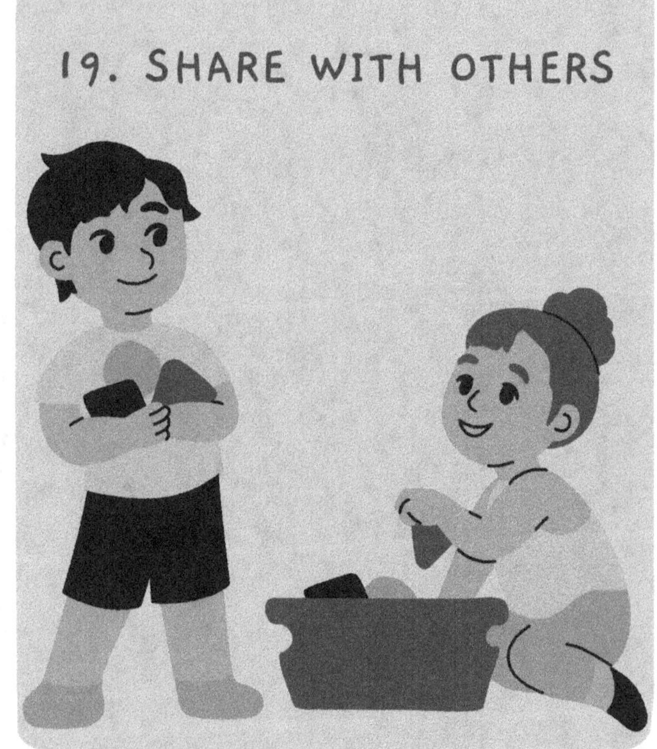

20. USE APPROPRIATE LANGUAGE
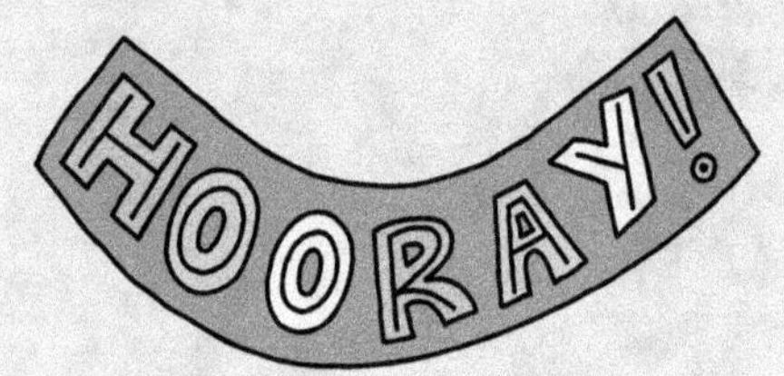

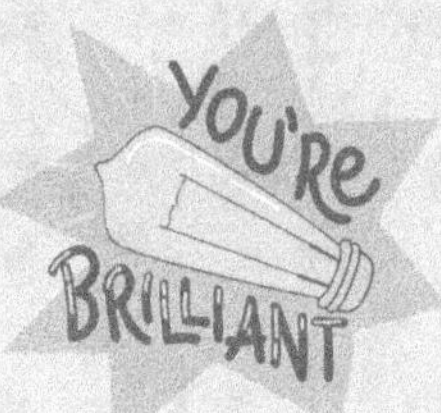

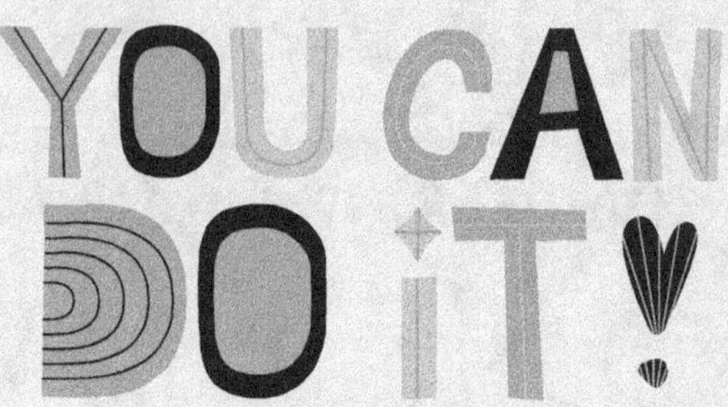

21. AVOID PUSHING OR SHOVING

22. WALK, DON'T RUN IN THE HALLWAYS

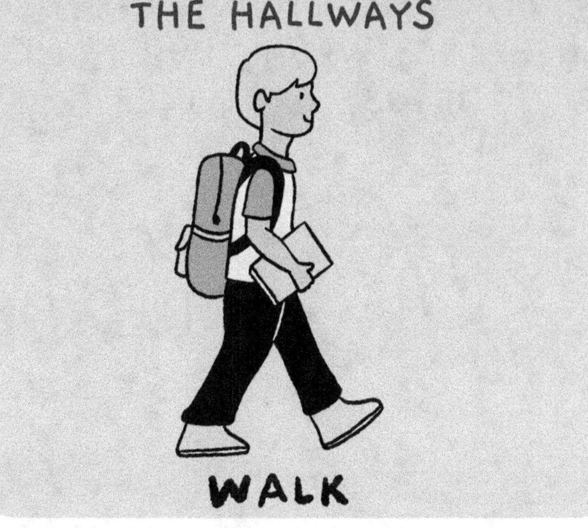

23. USE THE EQUIPMENT THE RIGHT WAY

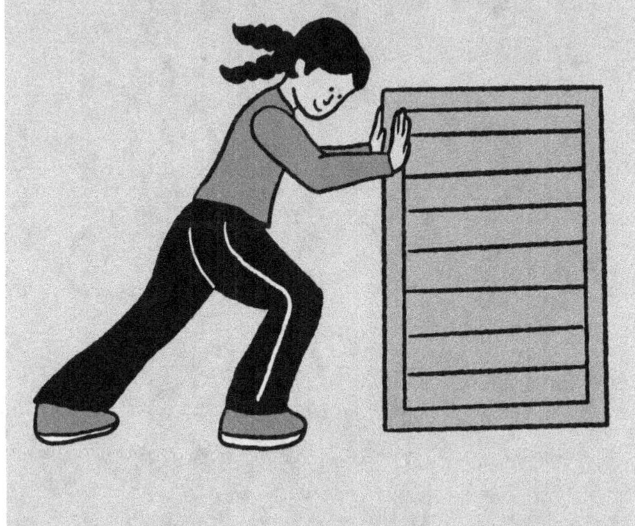

24. BE FRIENDLY AND RESPECTFUL

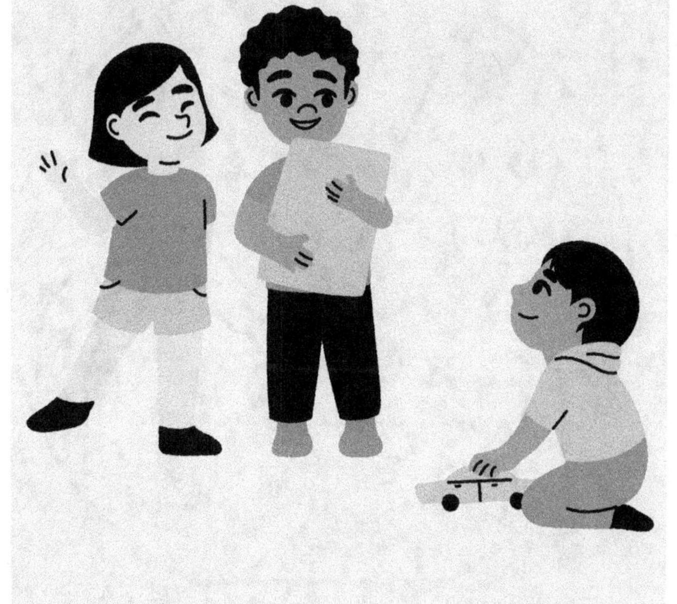

HYGIENE GENERAL RULES

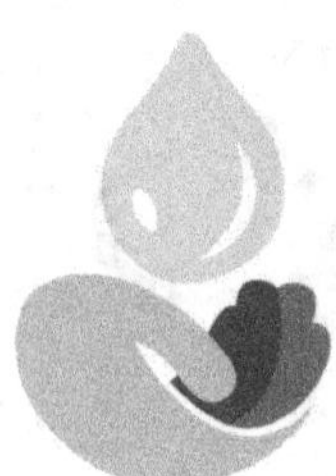
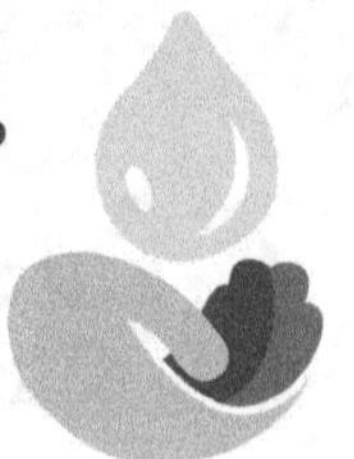

25. AFTER COUGHING OR SNEEZING, WASH YOUR HANDS OR USE SANITIZER

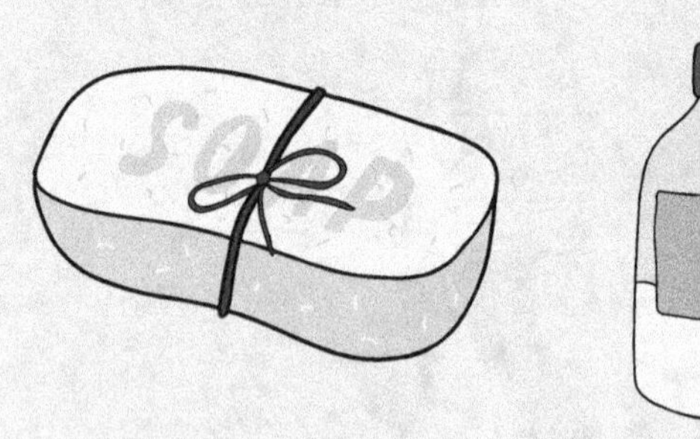

26. STAY HOME WHEN YOU DON'T FEEL WELL

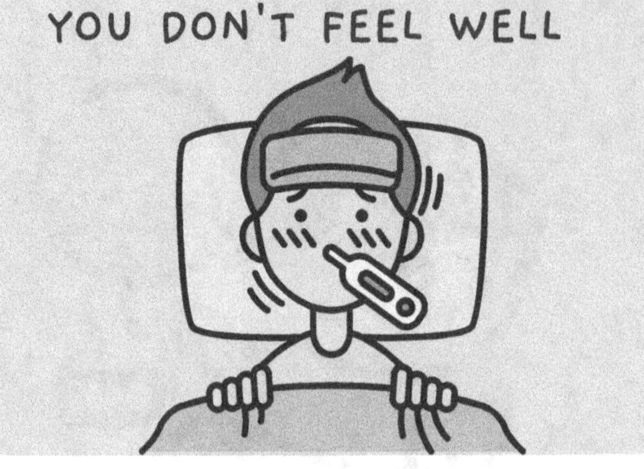

27. WASH YOUR HANDS FOR 20 SECONDS

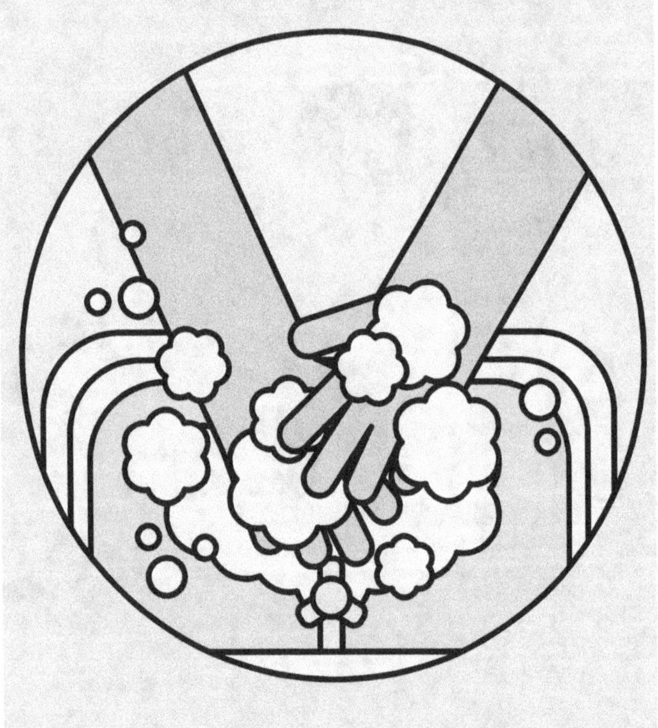

28. COVER YOUR MOUTH AND NOSE WHEN YOU COUGH OR SNEEZE

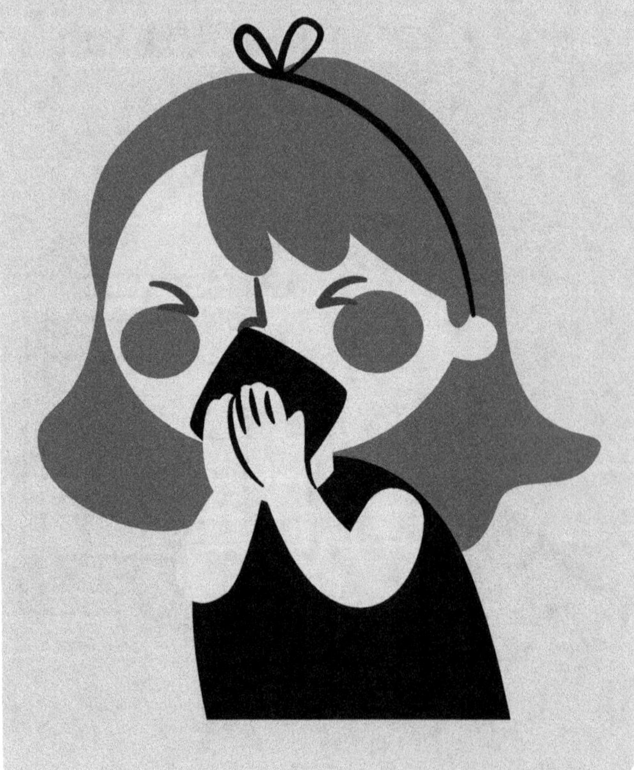

ACTIVITIES

Search and Find Class Rules

Color all the pictures that are following the rules.

Cross out the incorrect behaviors.

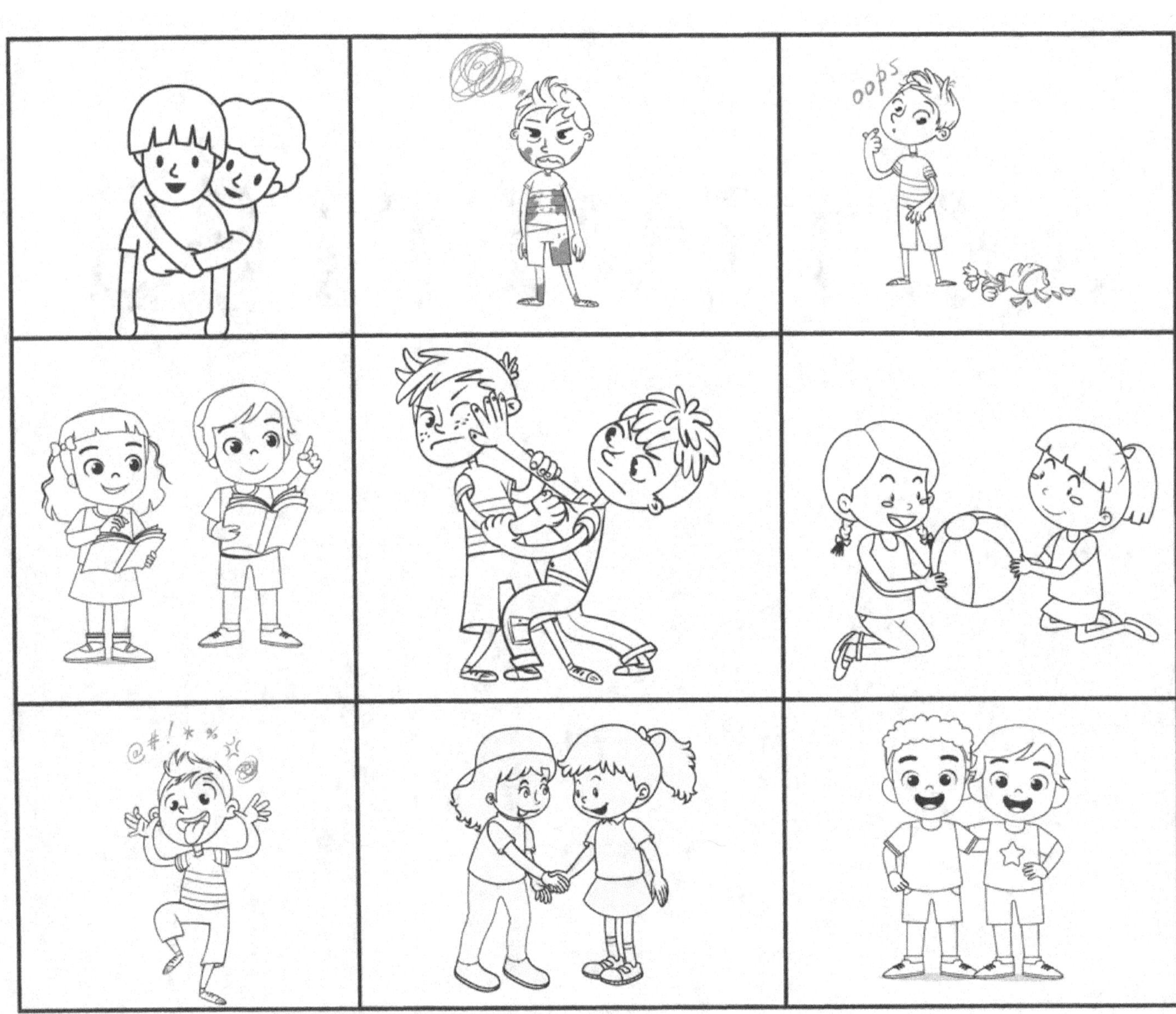

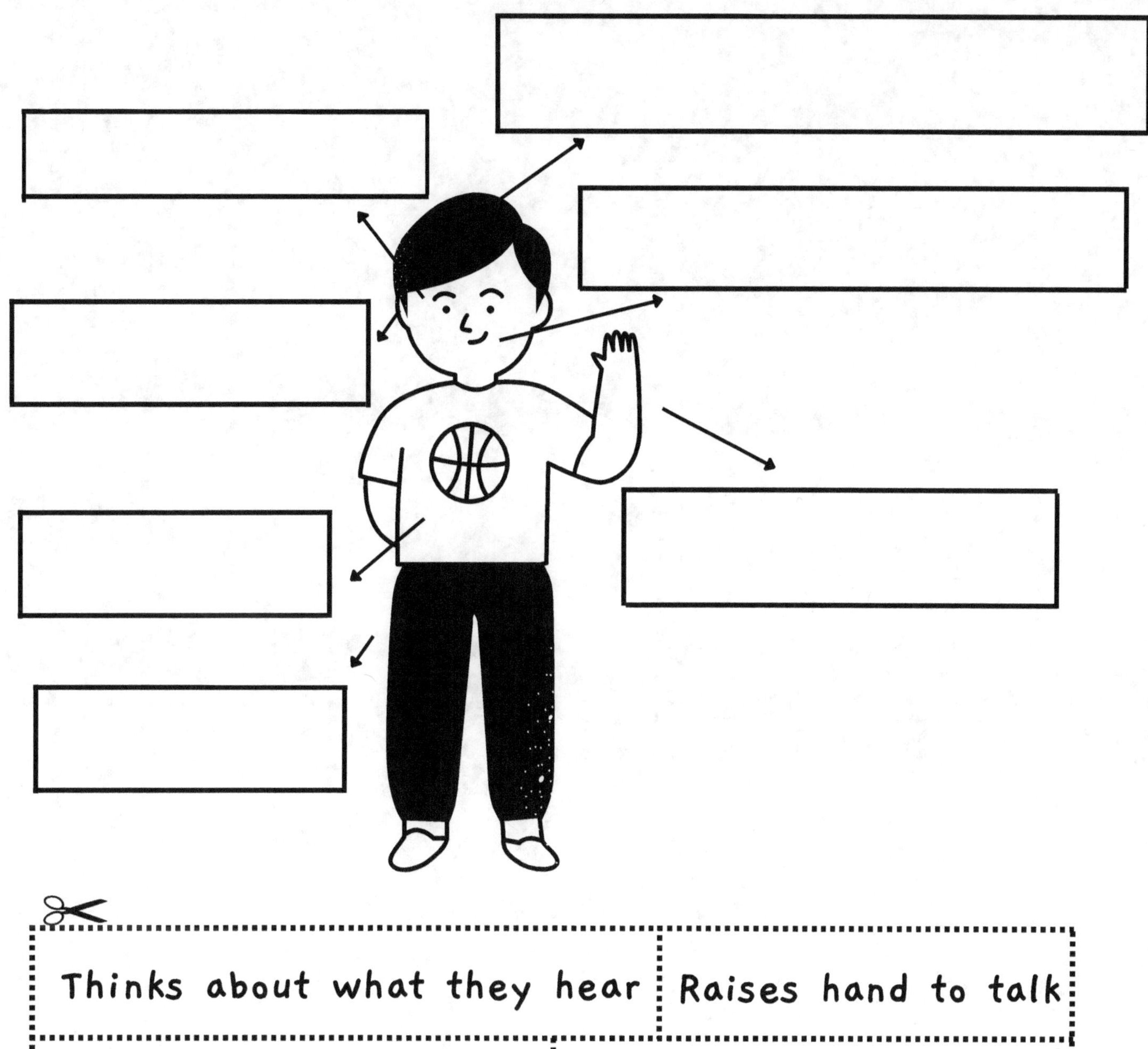

GOOD LISTENER

Cut out the boxes below and glue them in the correct part of the child

Search and Find Class Rules

Color all the pictures that are following the rules.

Cut them out and glue them to the next page.

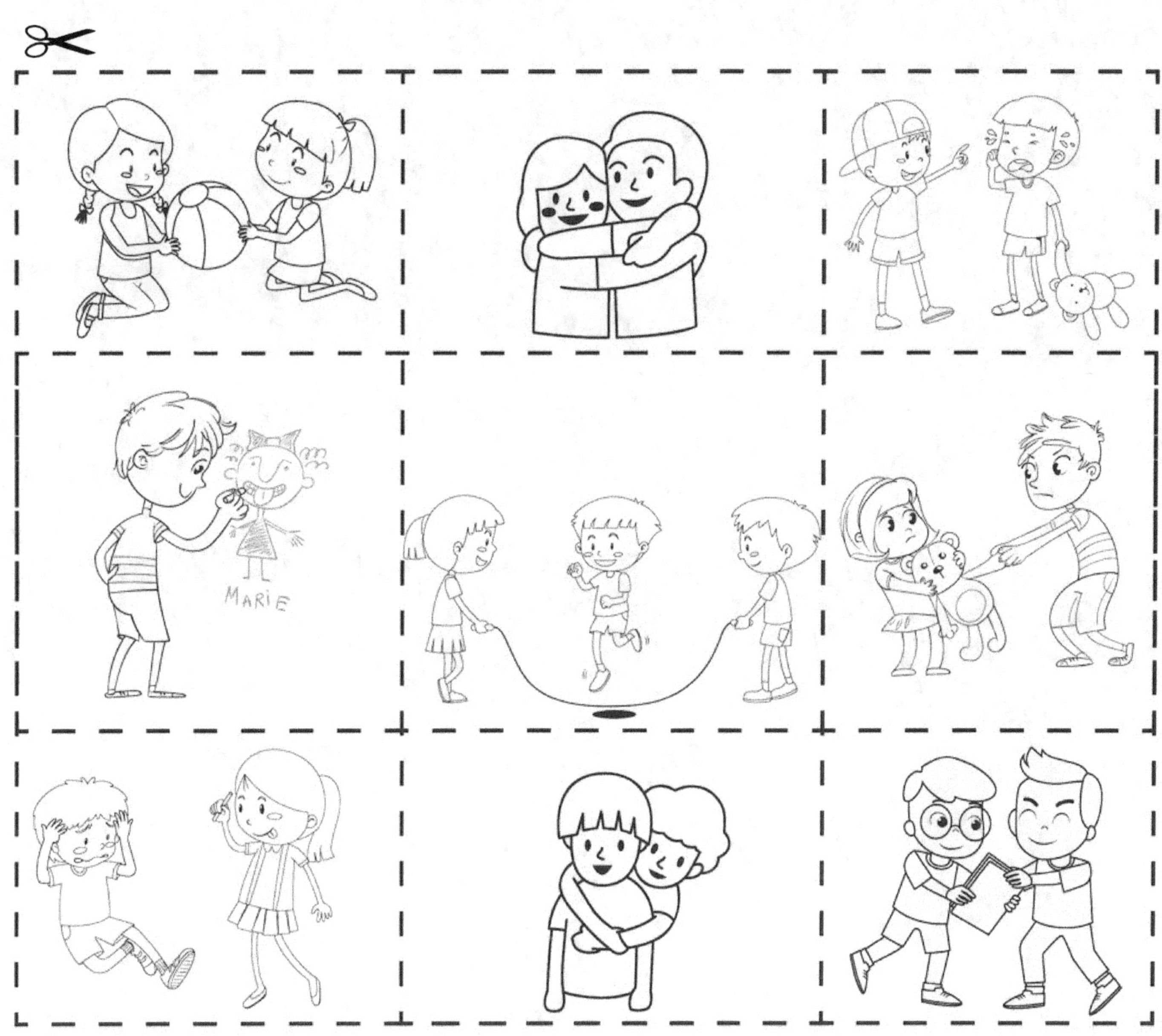

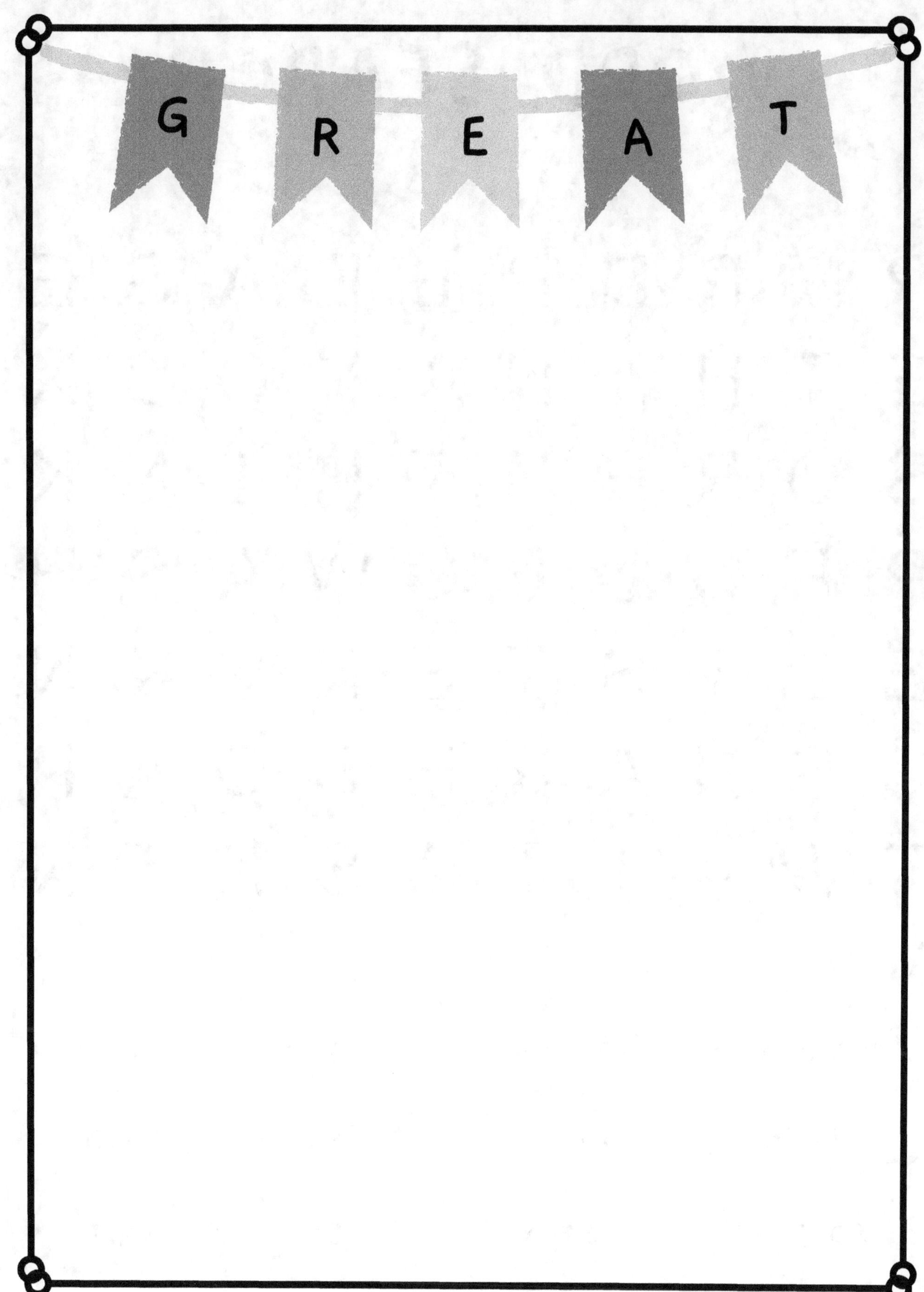
G R E A T

WORD SEARCH

```
R M R D P L E A S E
E T H A N K Y O U X
S O R R Y T H I N K
P F O L L O W A S H
E L I S T E N V K N
C S H A R E S O A P
T W A I T A S K T N
```

THANK YOU	FOLLOW	THINK	SHARE
PLEASE	SOAP	RESPECT	WASH
SORRY	LISTEN	ASK	WAIT

Complete the sentences using must or musn't

You _______ respect your
teacher

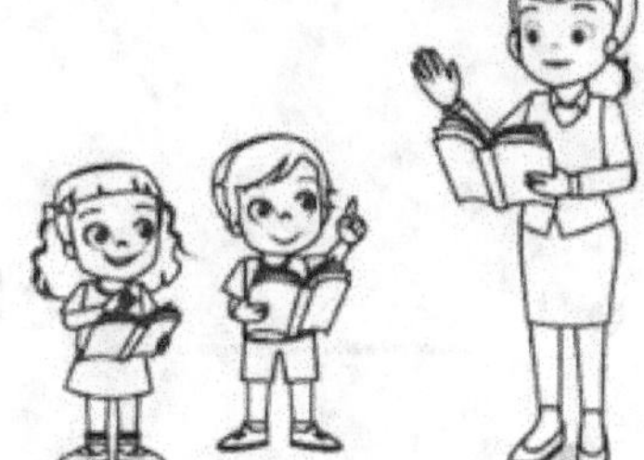

You _______ run in the
hallways

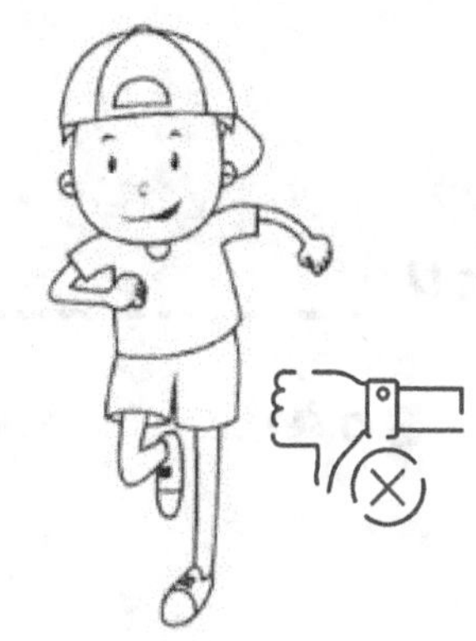

You _______ be disrespecrful

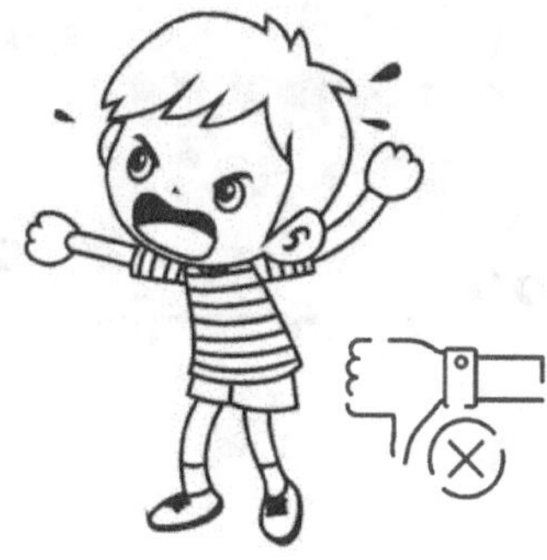

You _______ wash your hand for
20 seconds

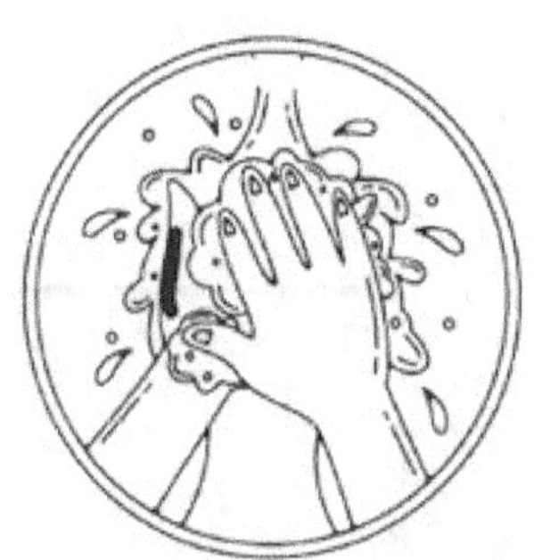

Complete the senteces using must or musn't

You _______ cheat

You _______ raise your hand to speak

You _______ follow directions

You _______ scream

Draw a rule you like and why it is important

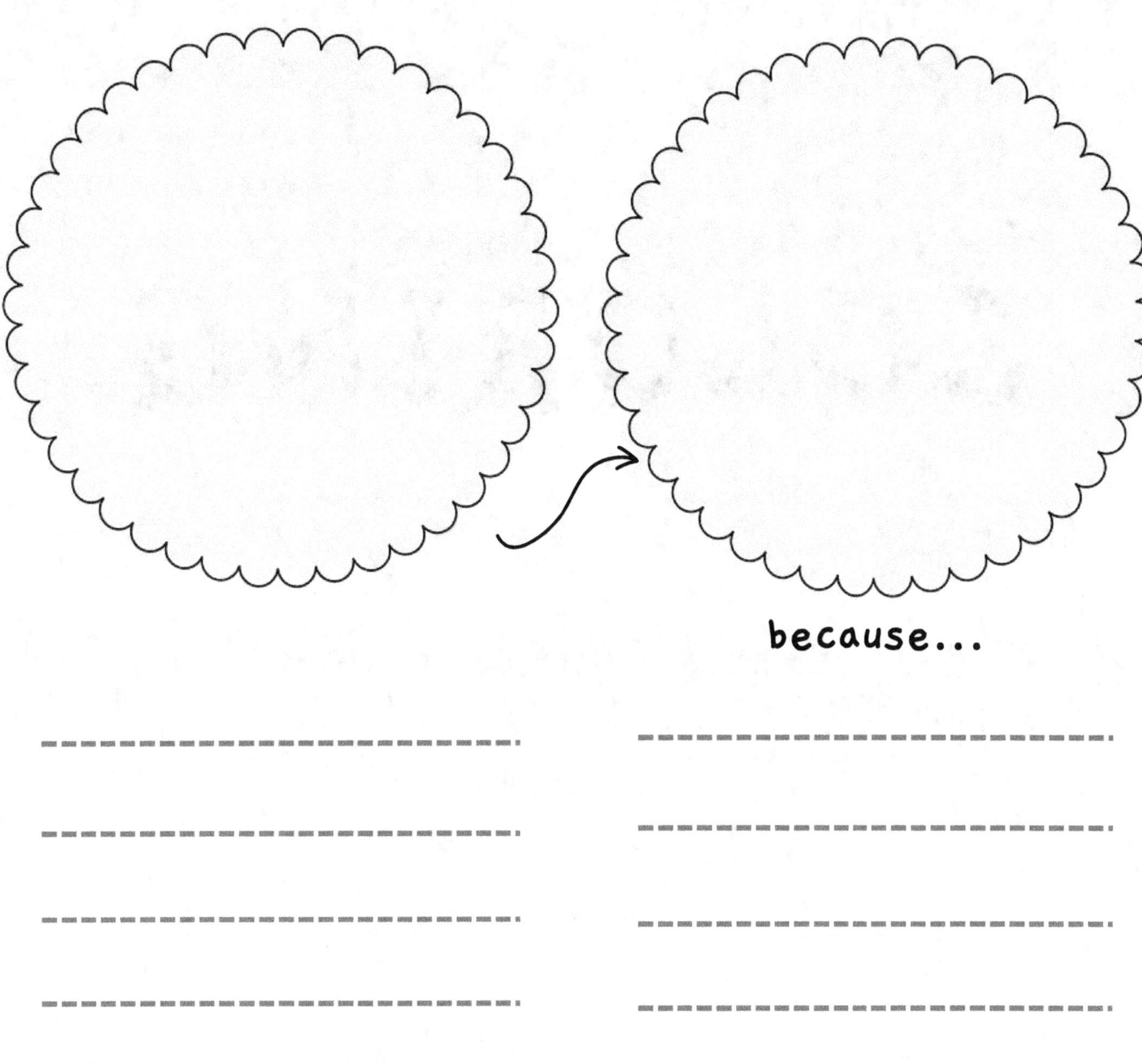

COLORING

Listen to the speaker

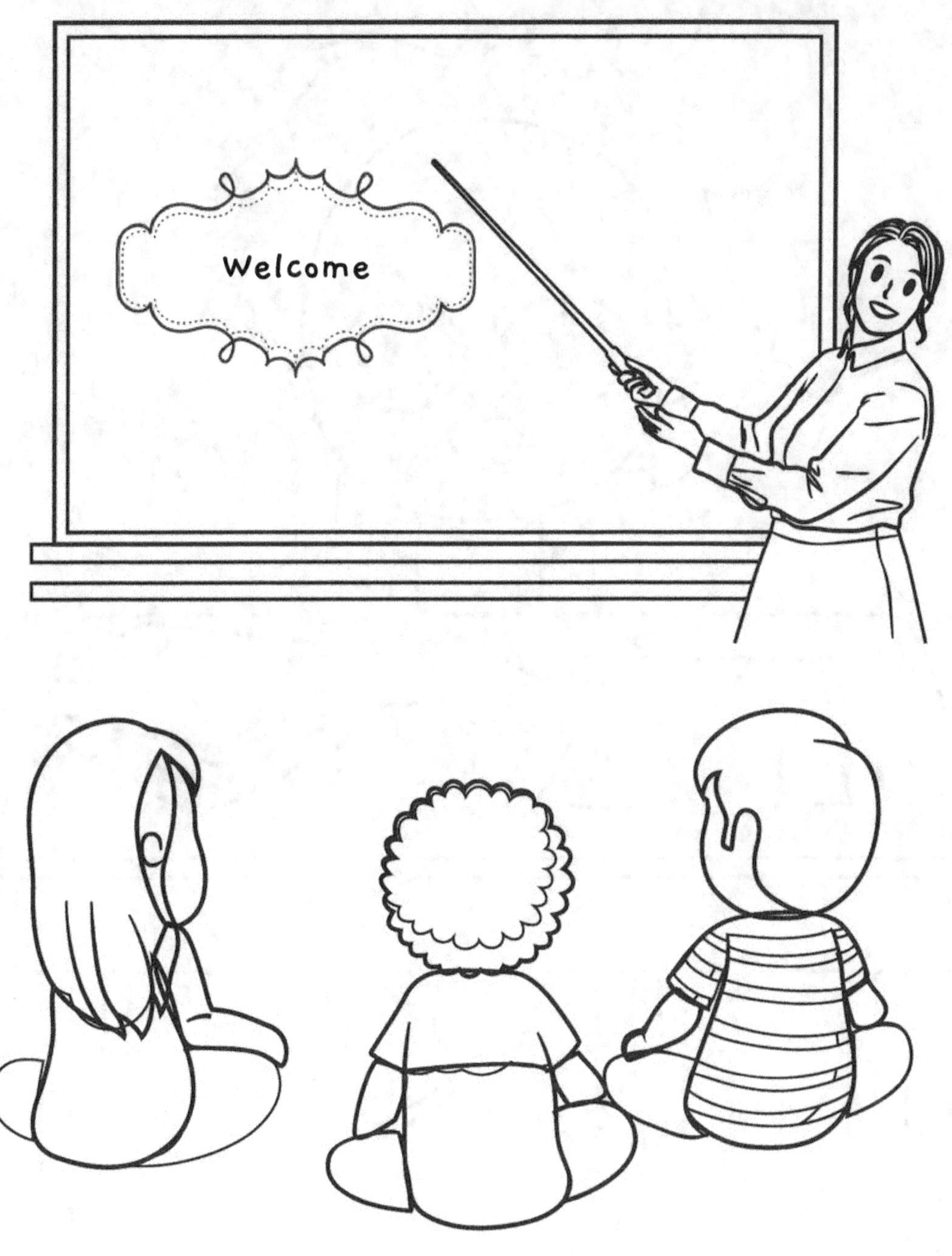

Raise your hand to speak

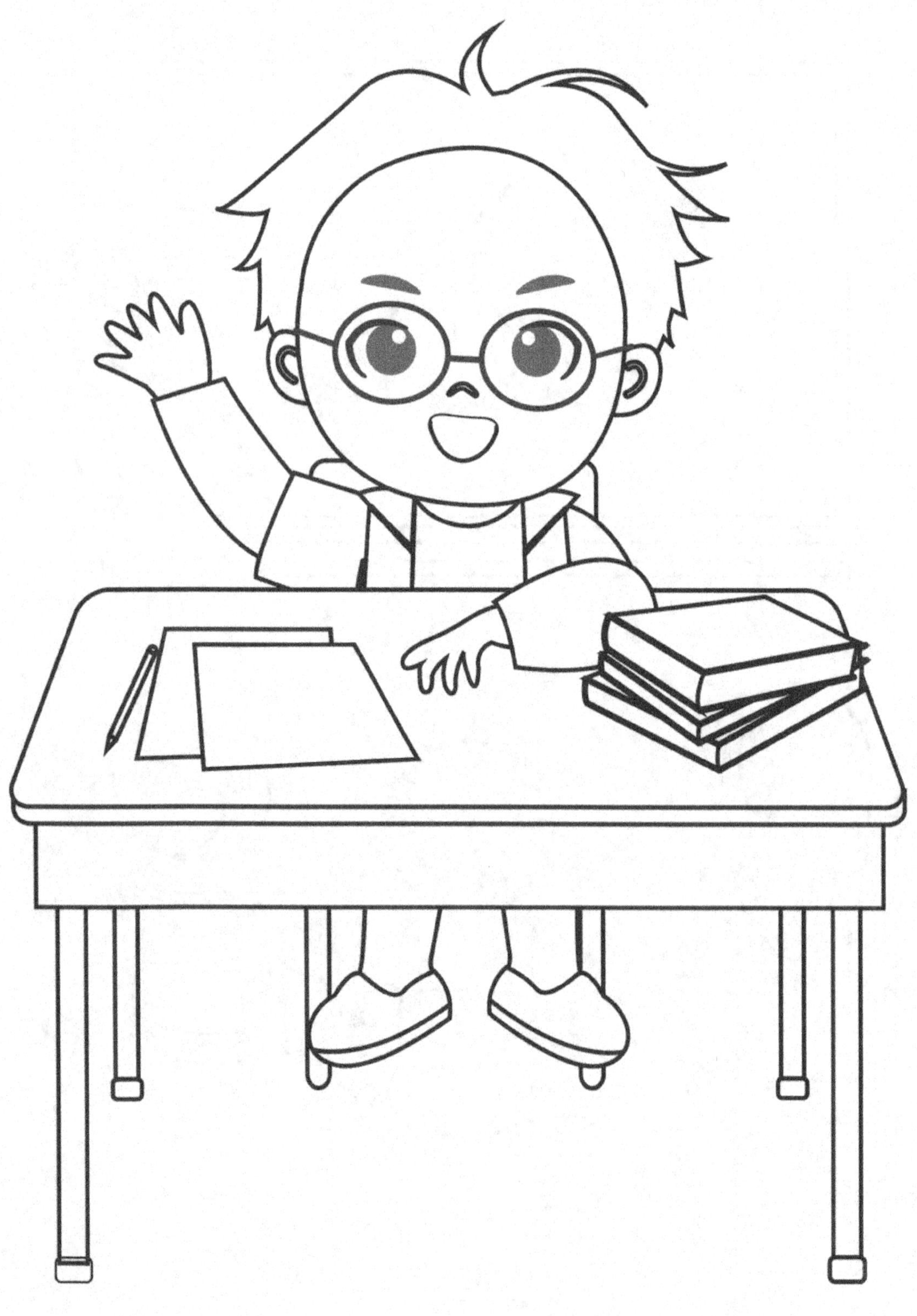

Respect your classmates and teacher

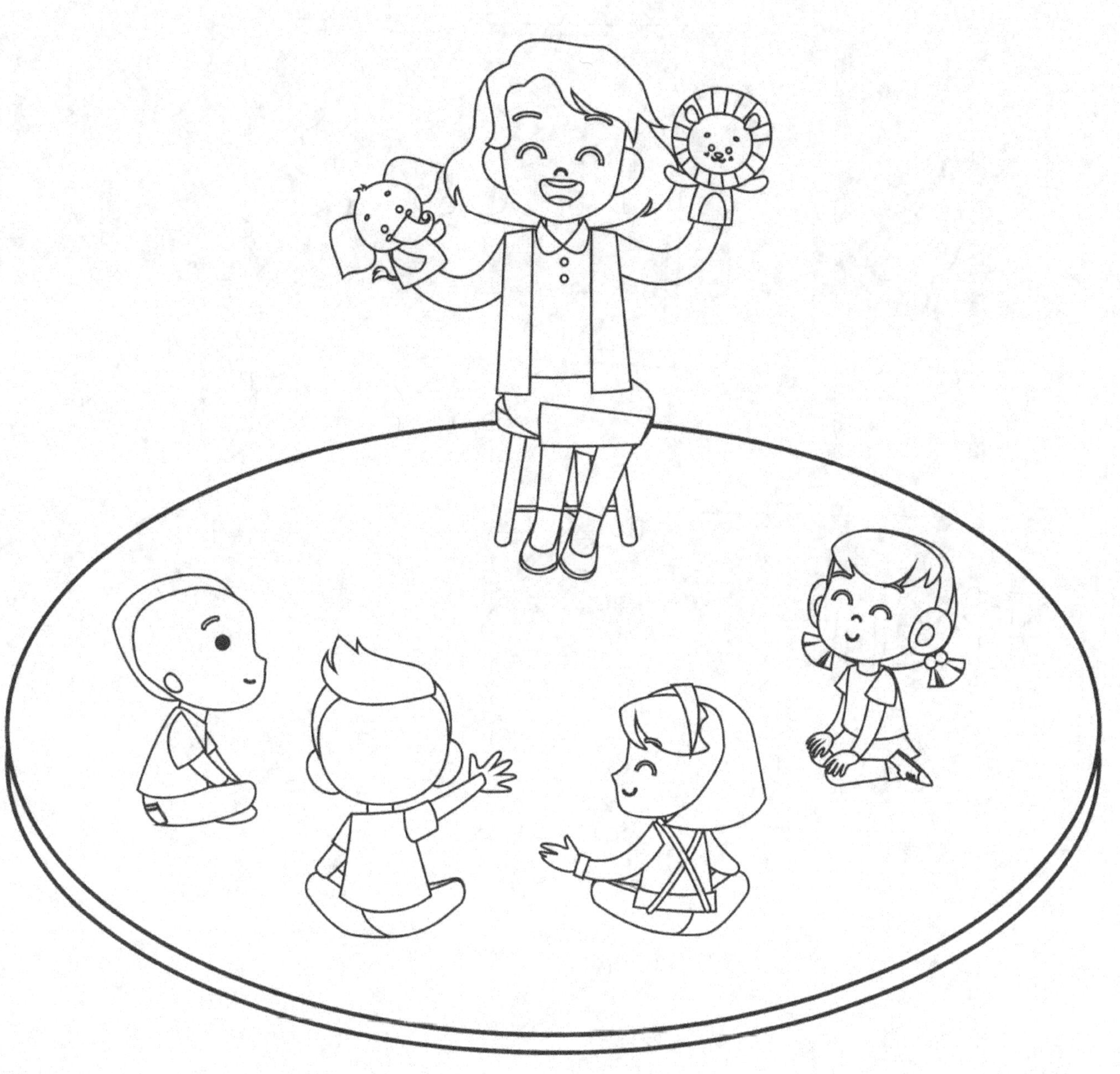

Say Please and Thank you

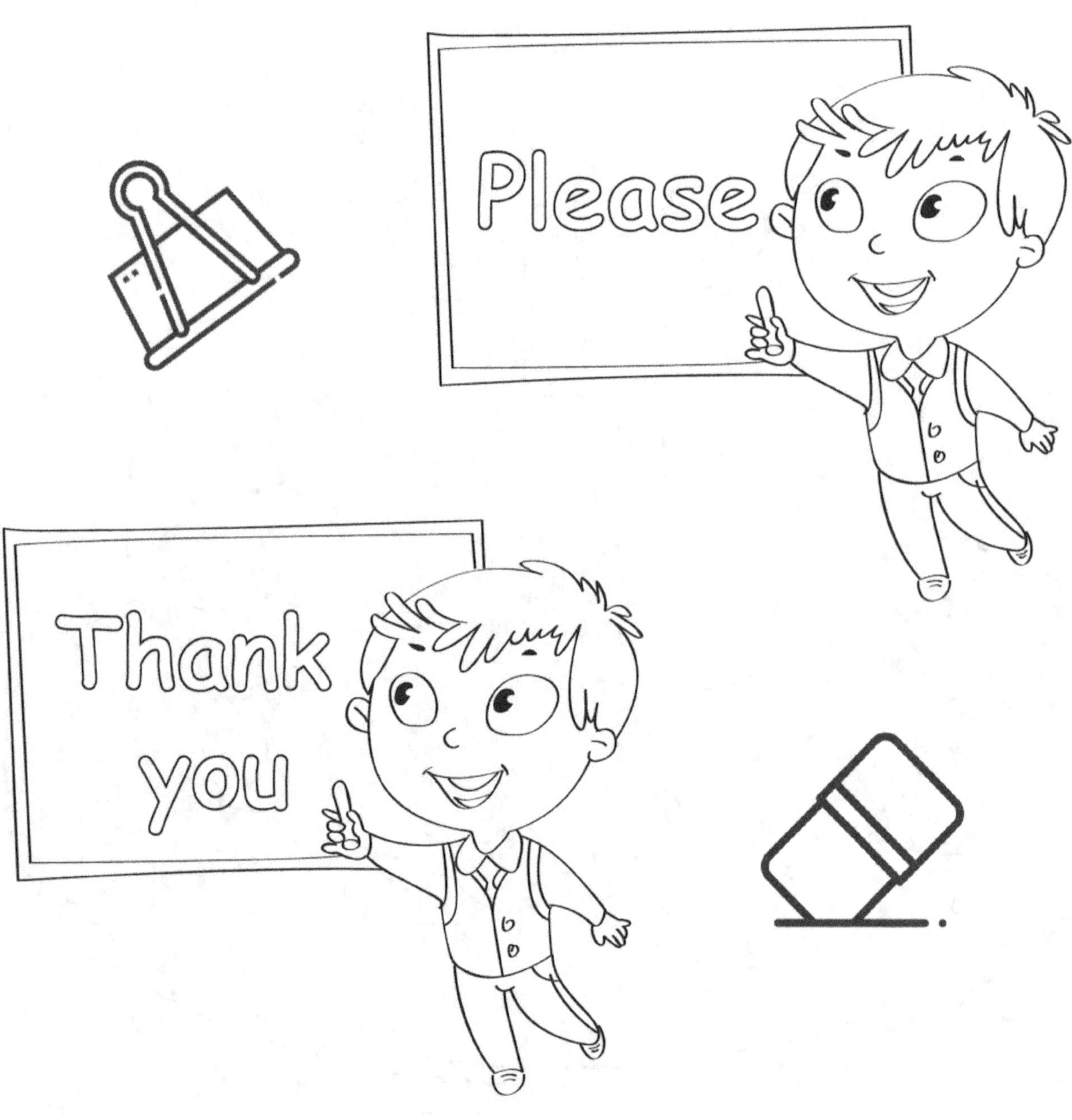

Follow
directions

Keep your hands to yourself

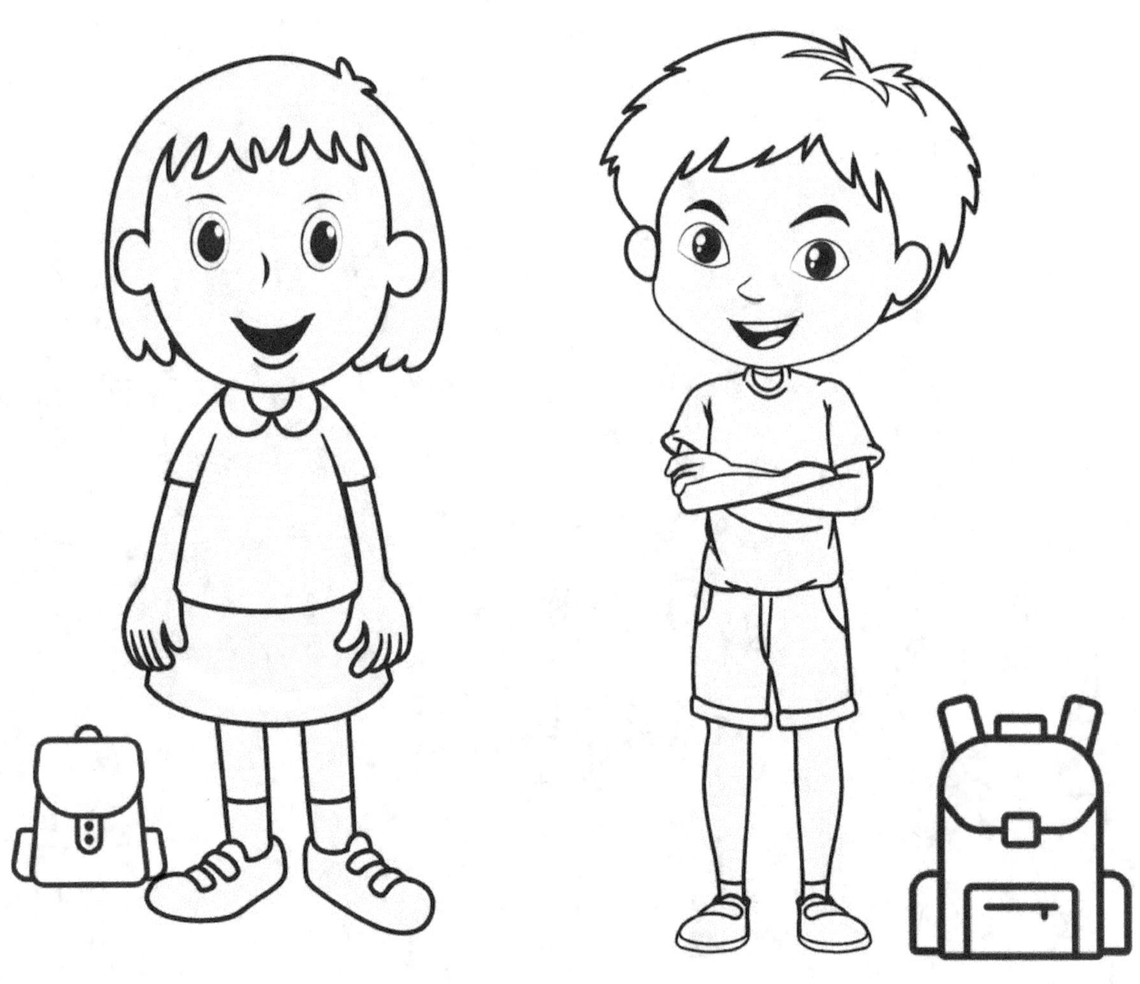

We Don't cheat

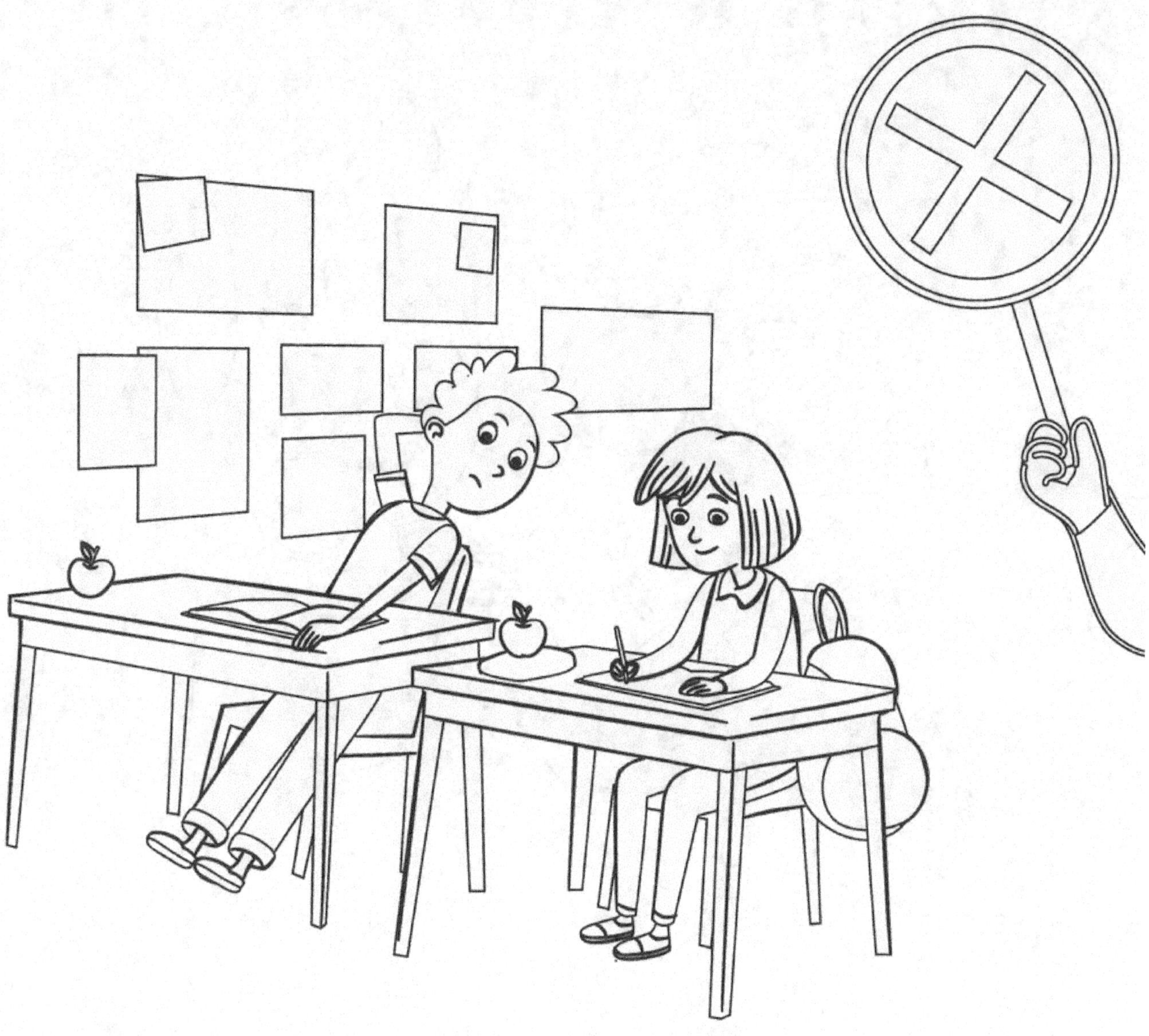

Help each other

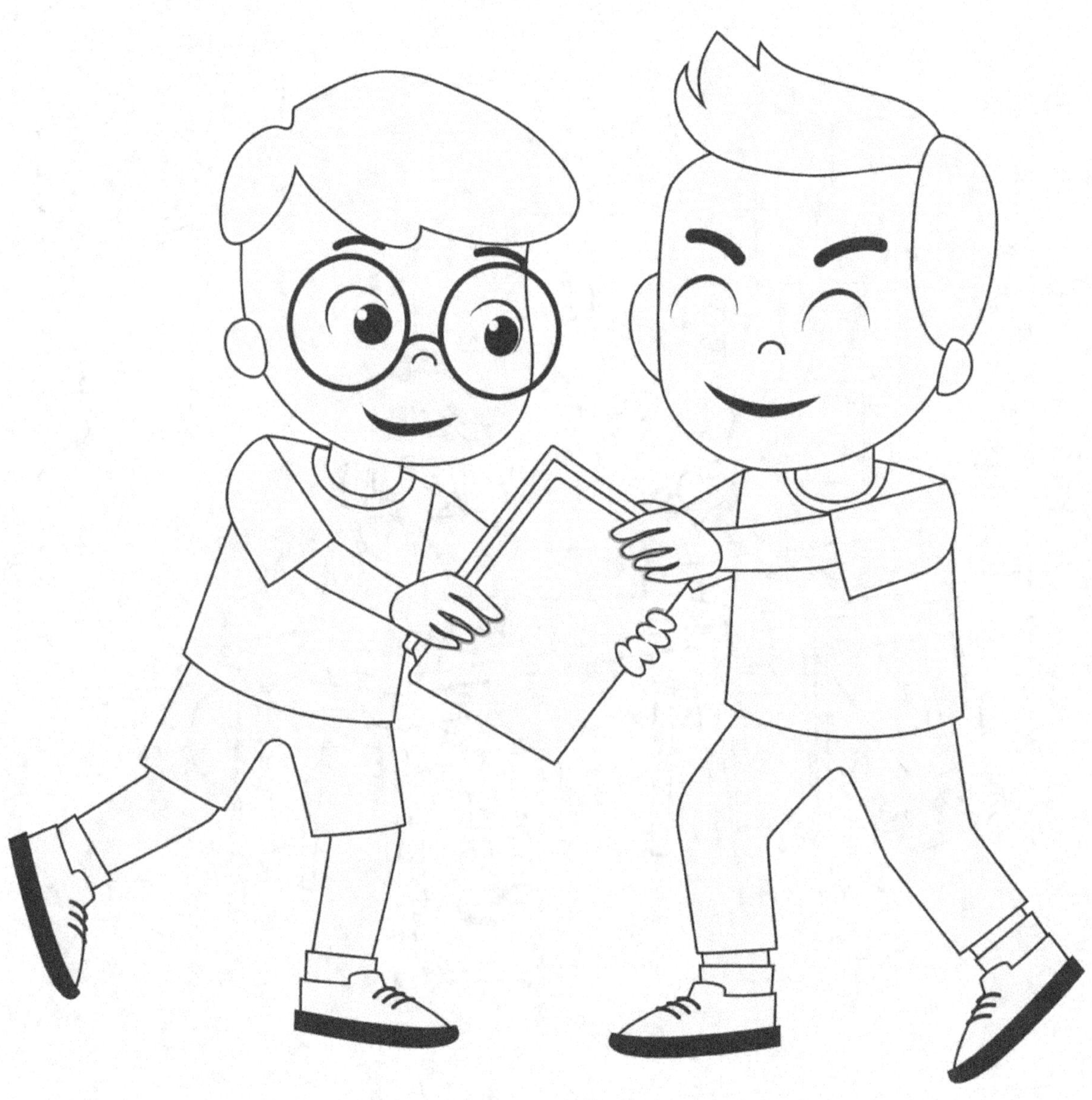

Use kind words

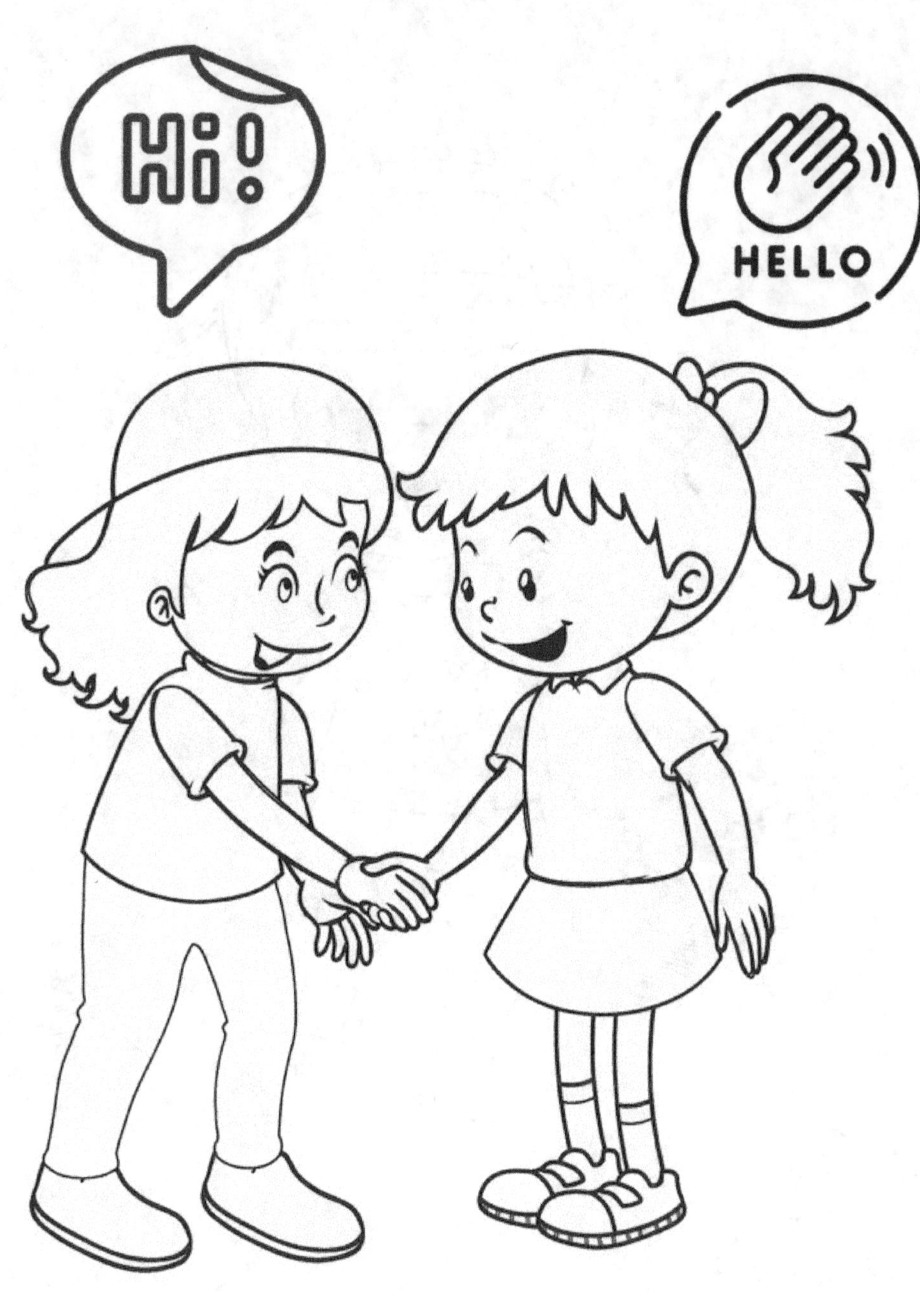

We speak softly in class

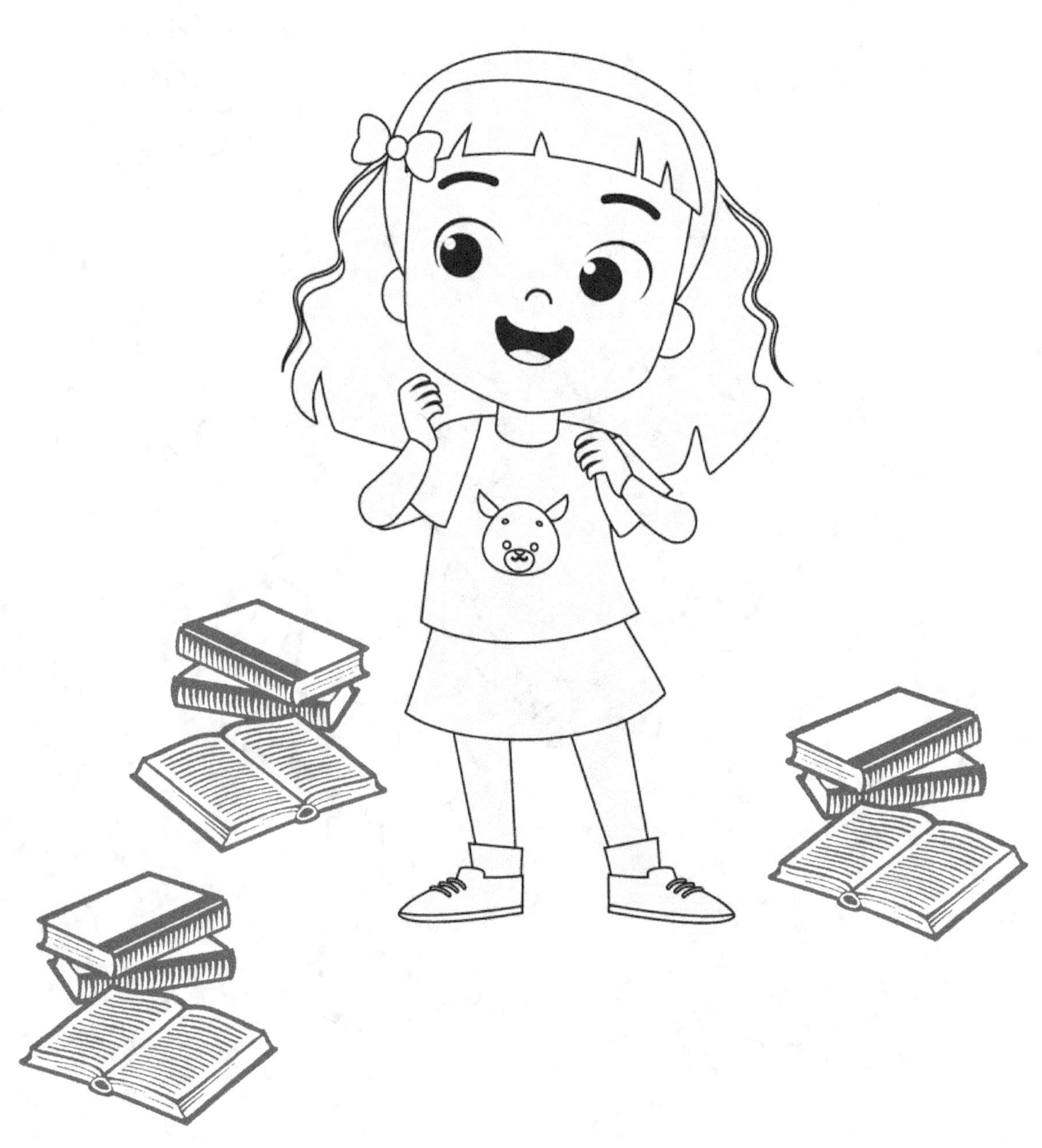

Respect others' property

Use technology appropriately

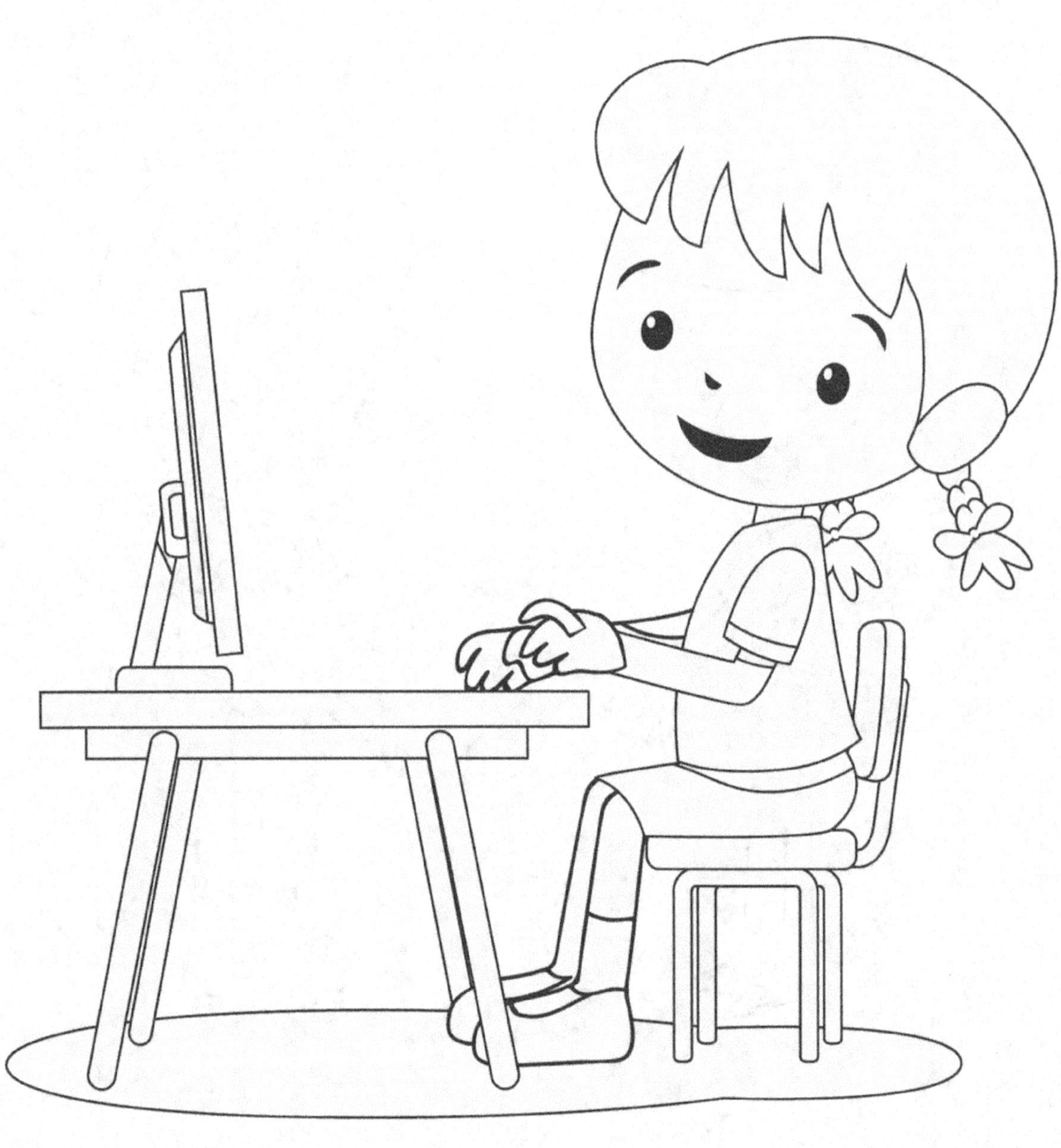

If you make a mess, clean it up

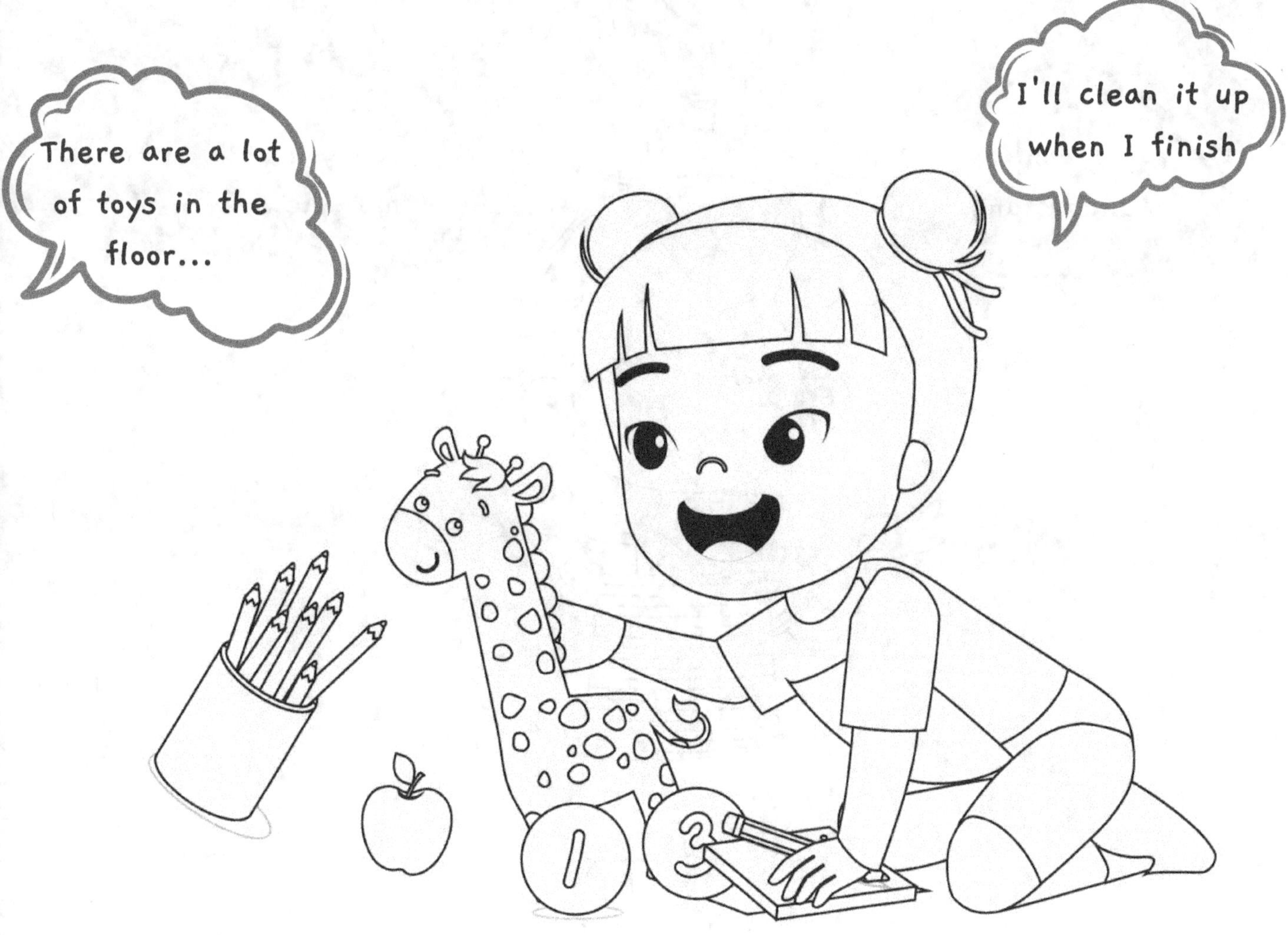

Always ask for help if you need it

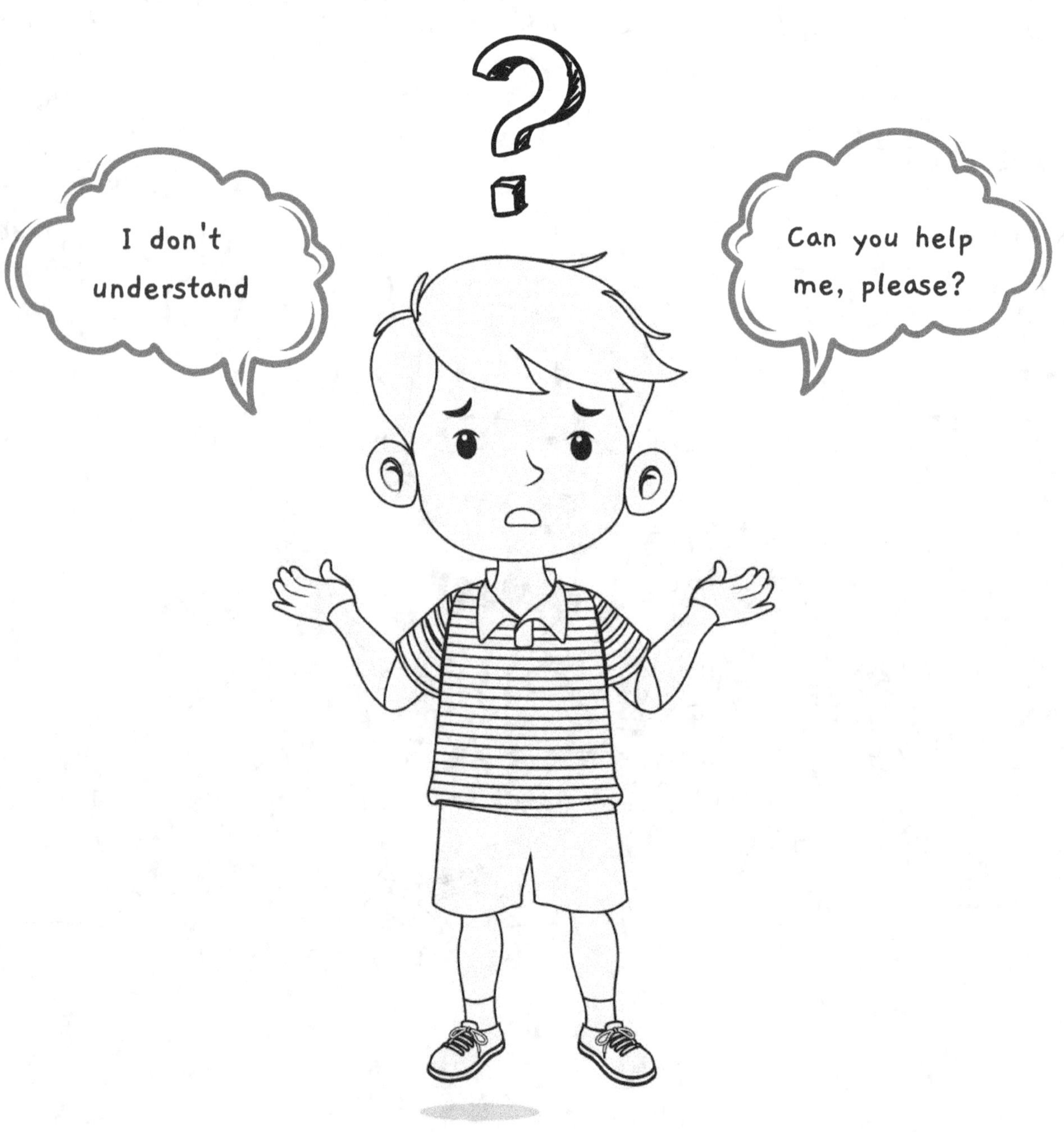

If you see someone in danger, tell an adult

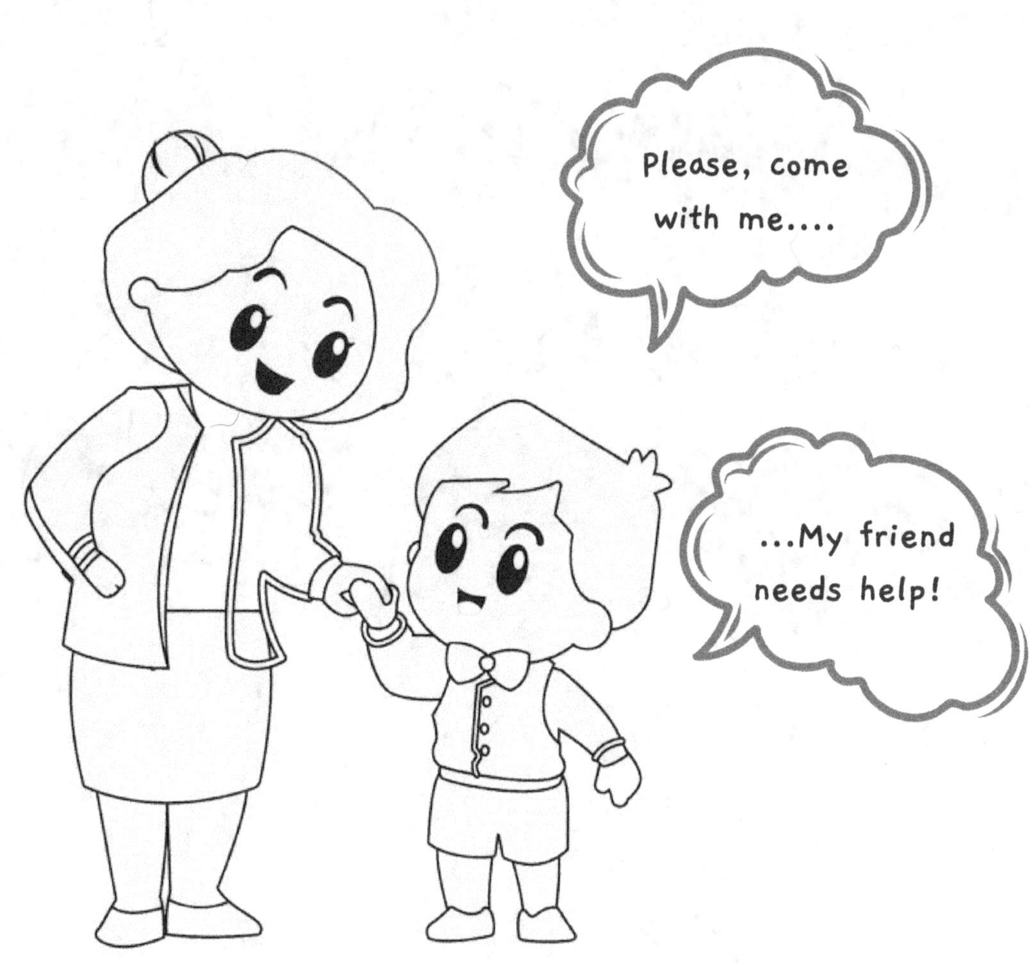

Be safe on the playground

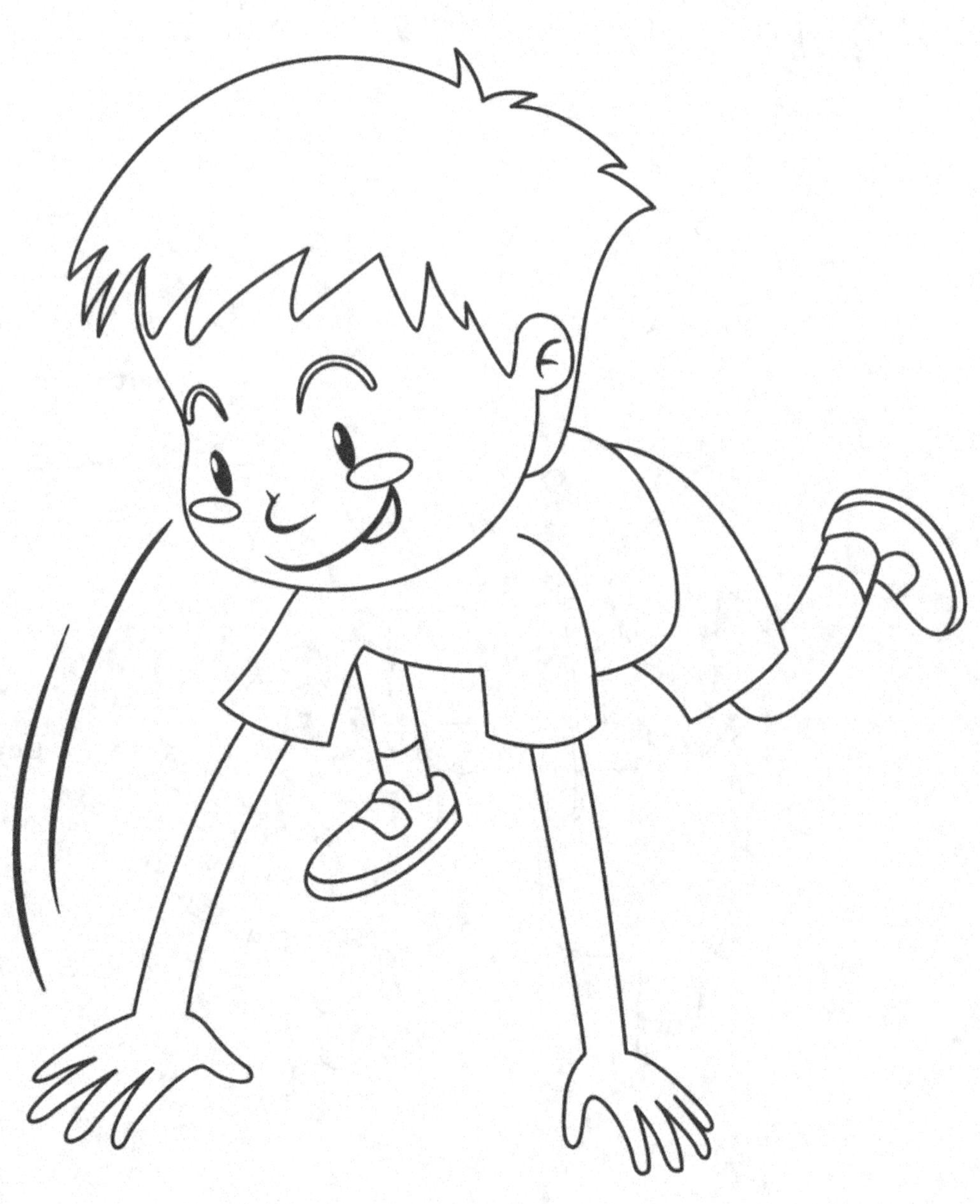

Wait your turn

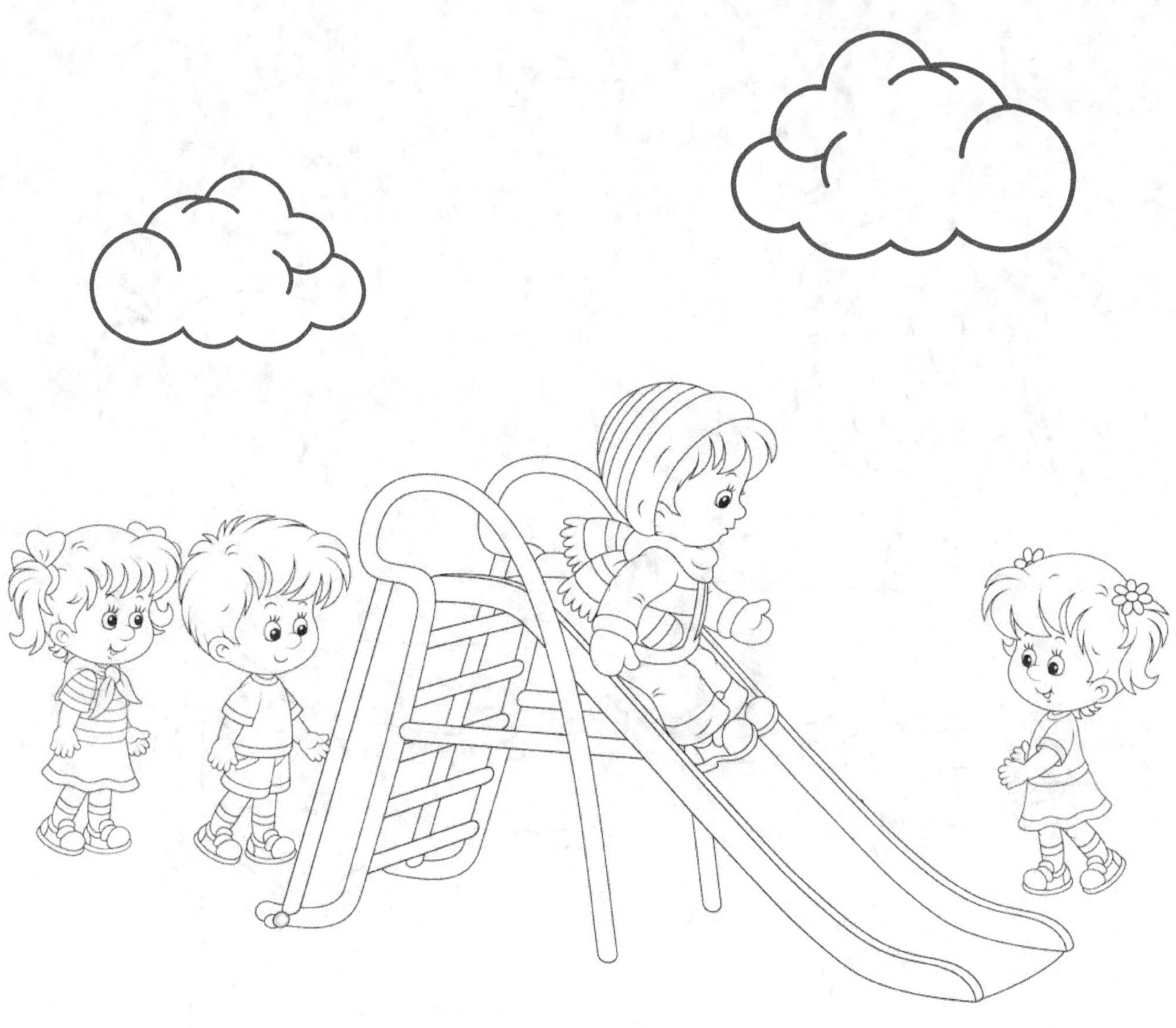

I will share

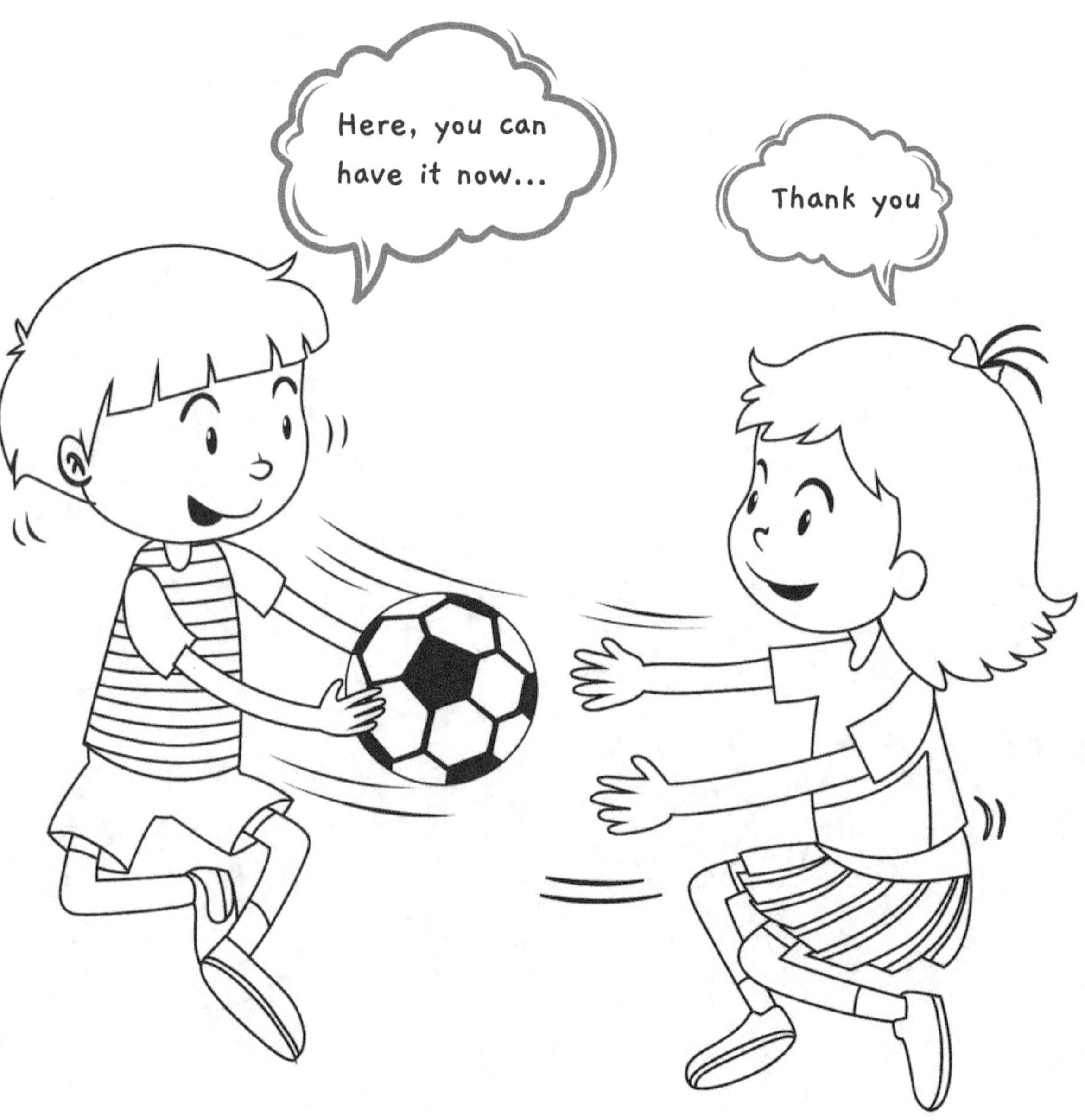

Play fair

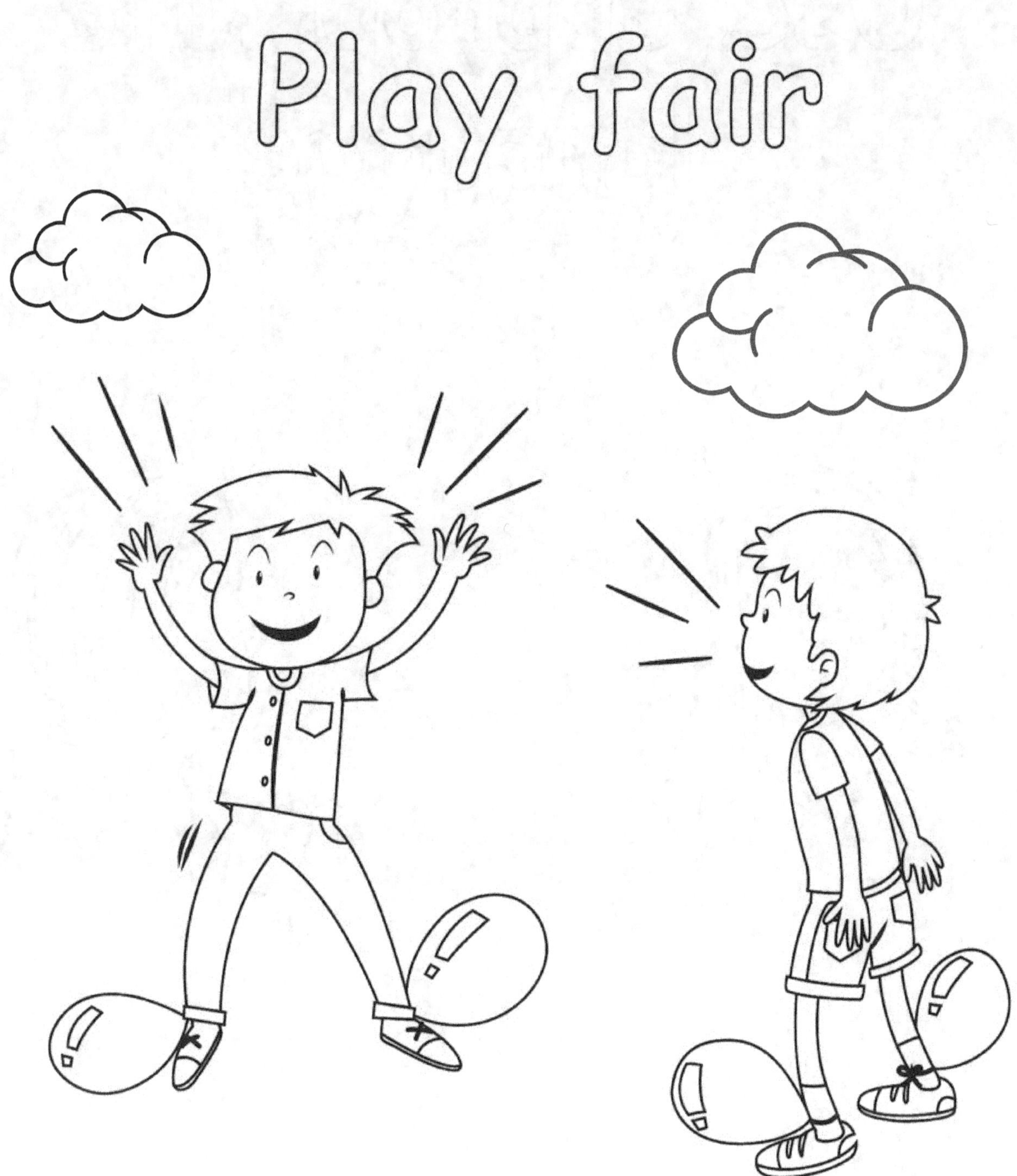

Use appropriate language

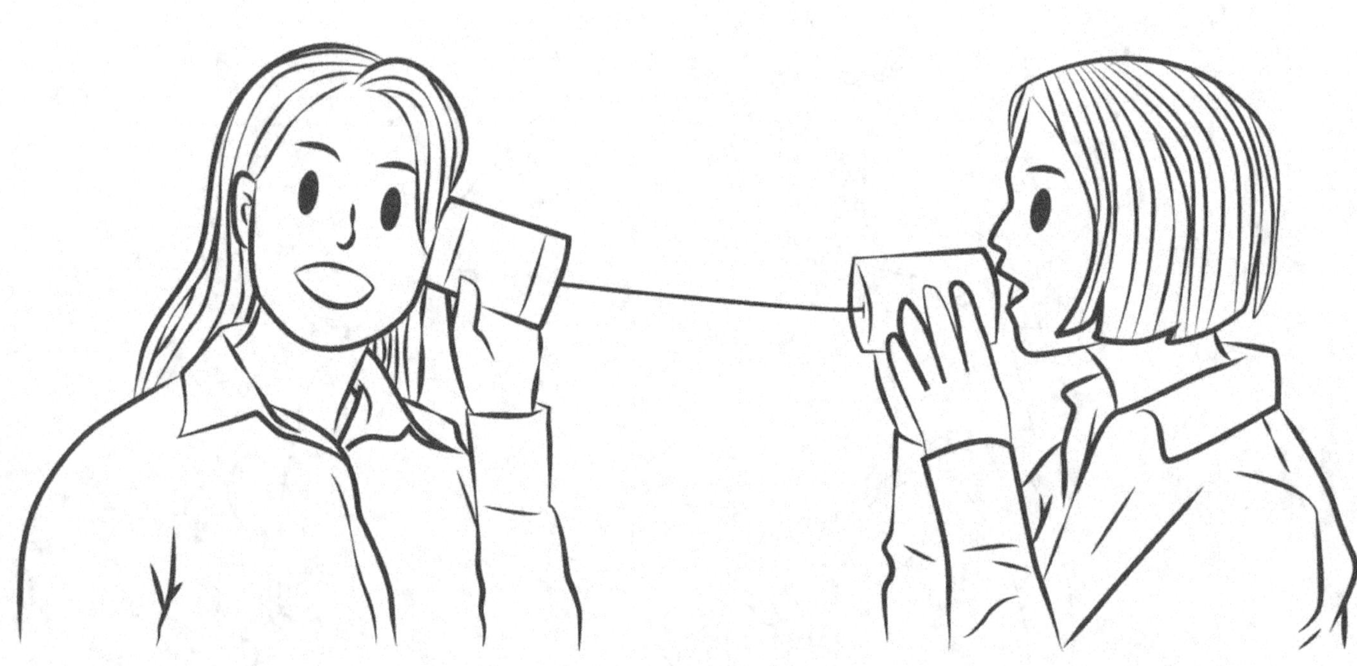

Be friendly and respectful

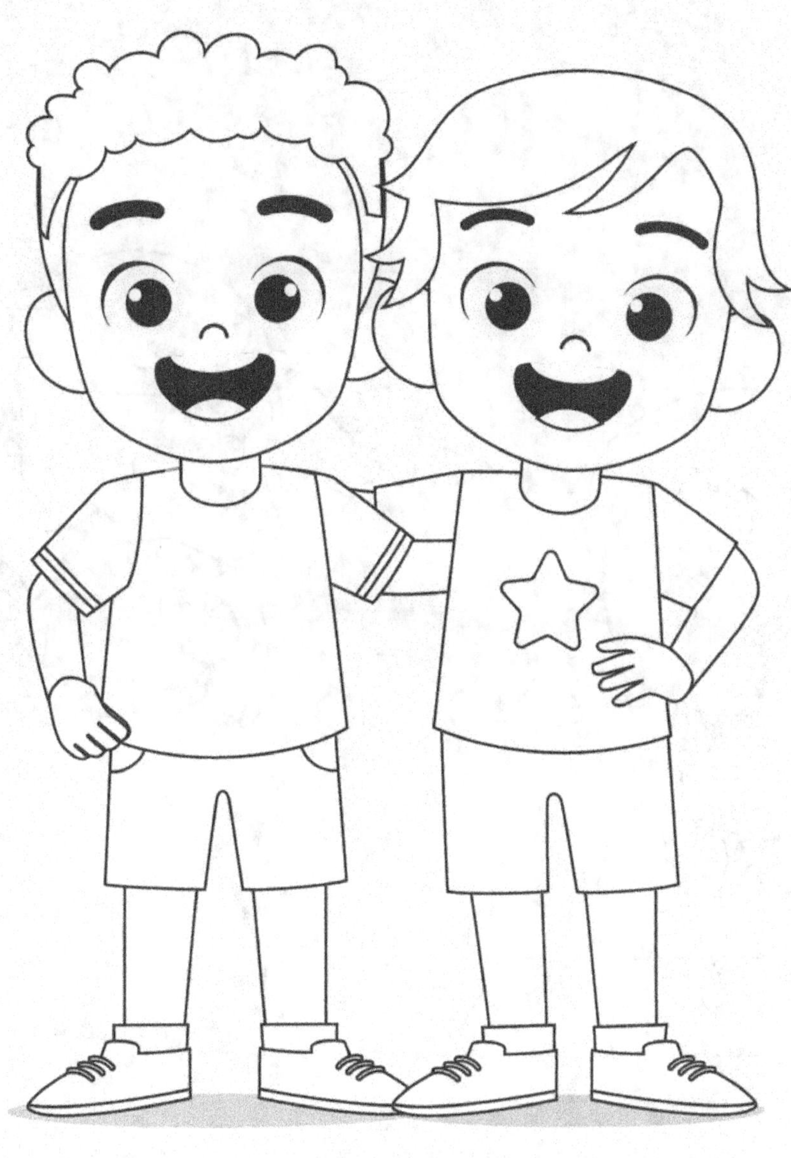

Use the equipment the right way

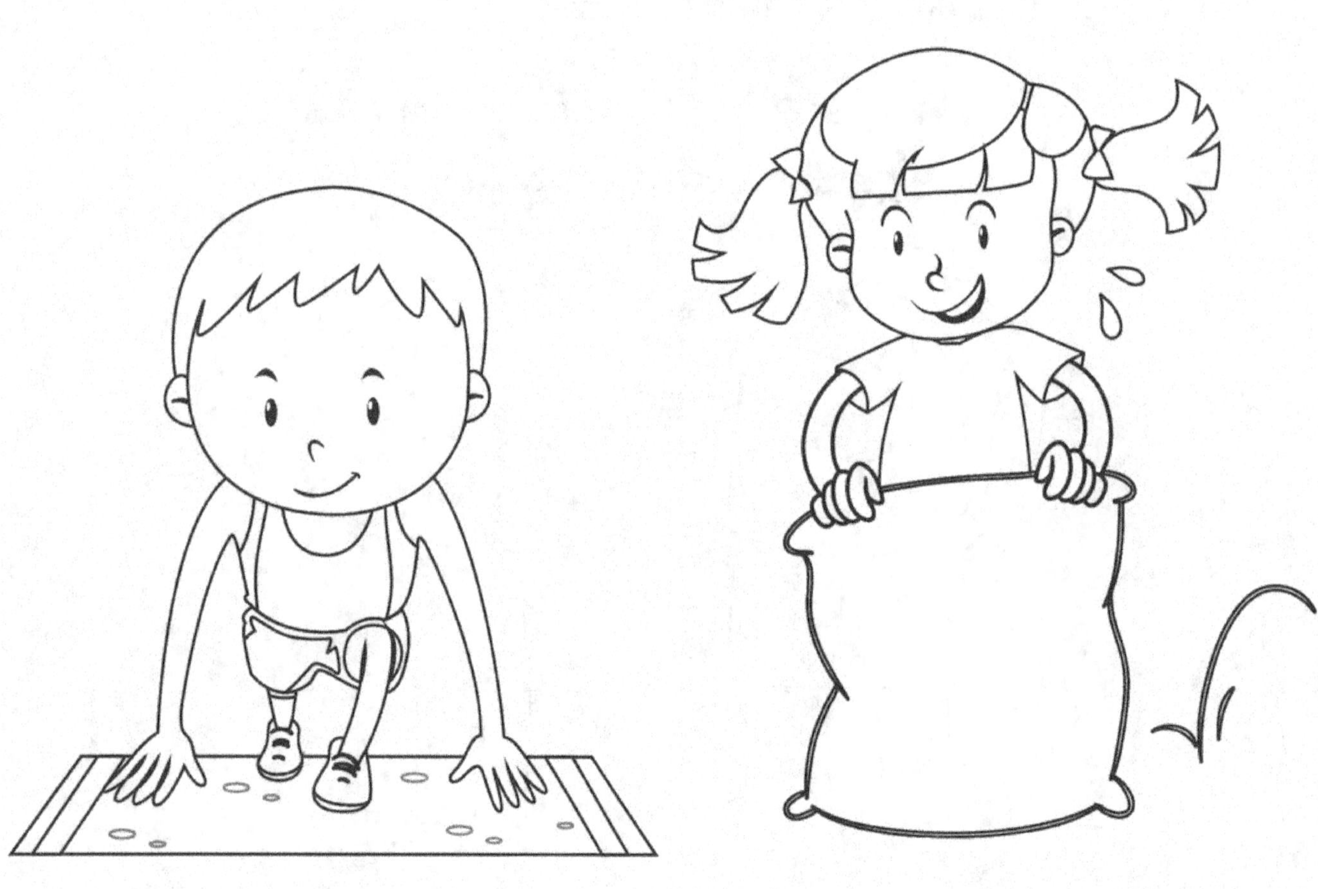

Do wash your hands
with soap or use Sanitizer

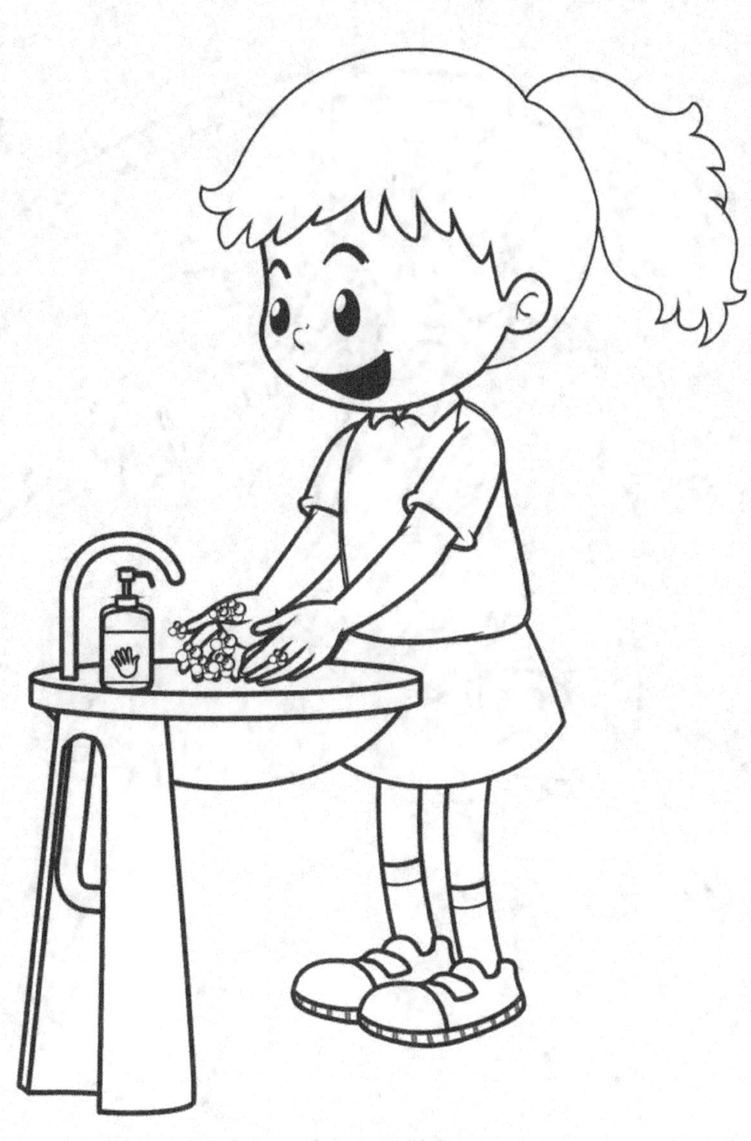

Do wash your hands for 20 seconds

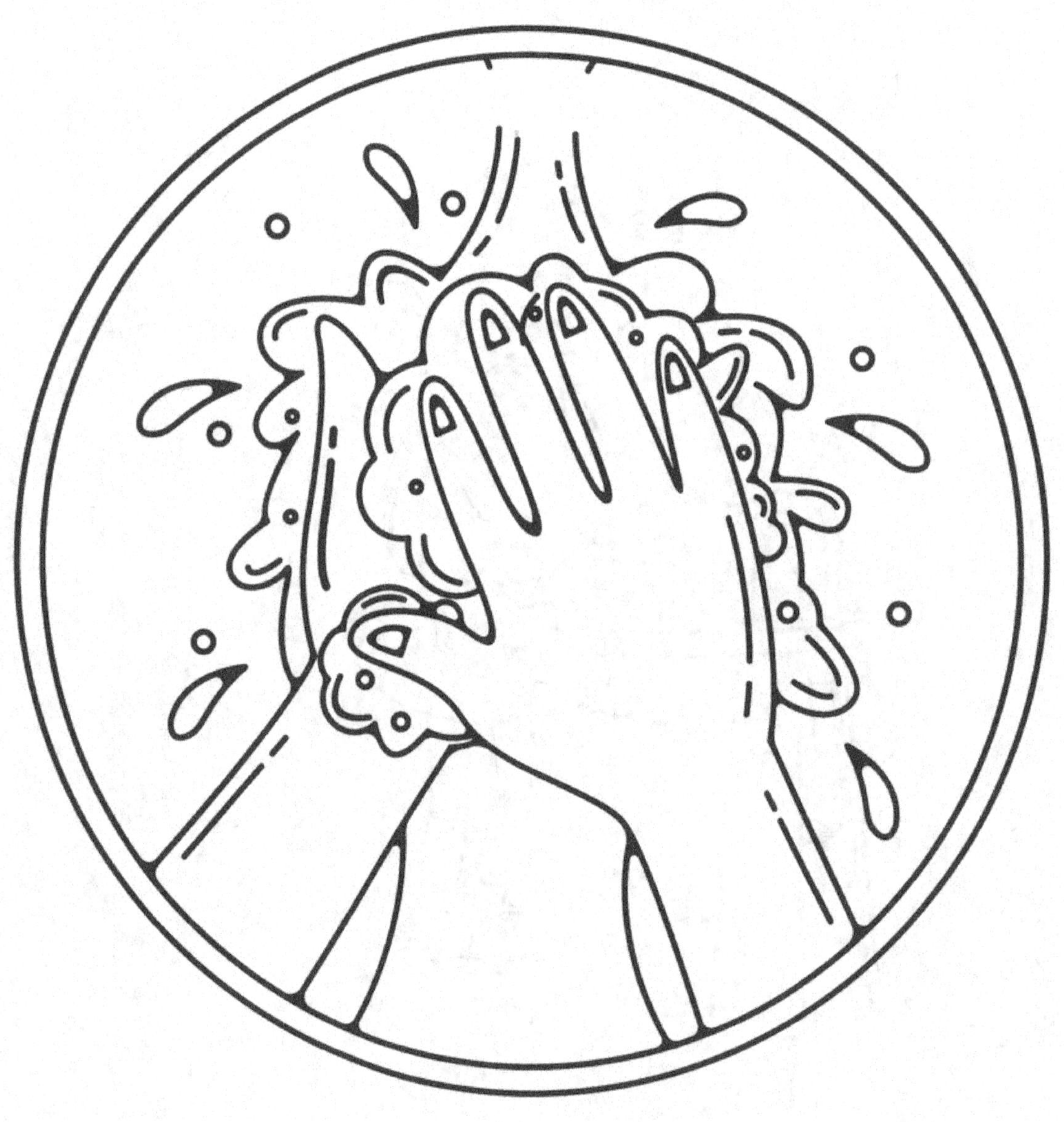

Do stay home when you don't feel well

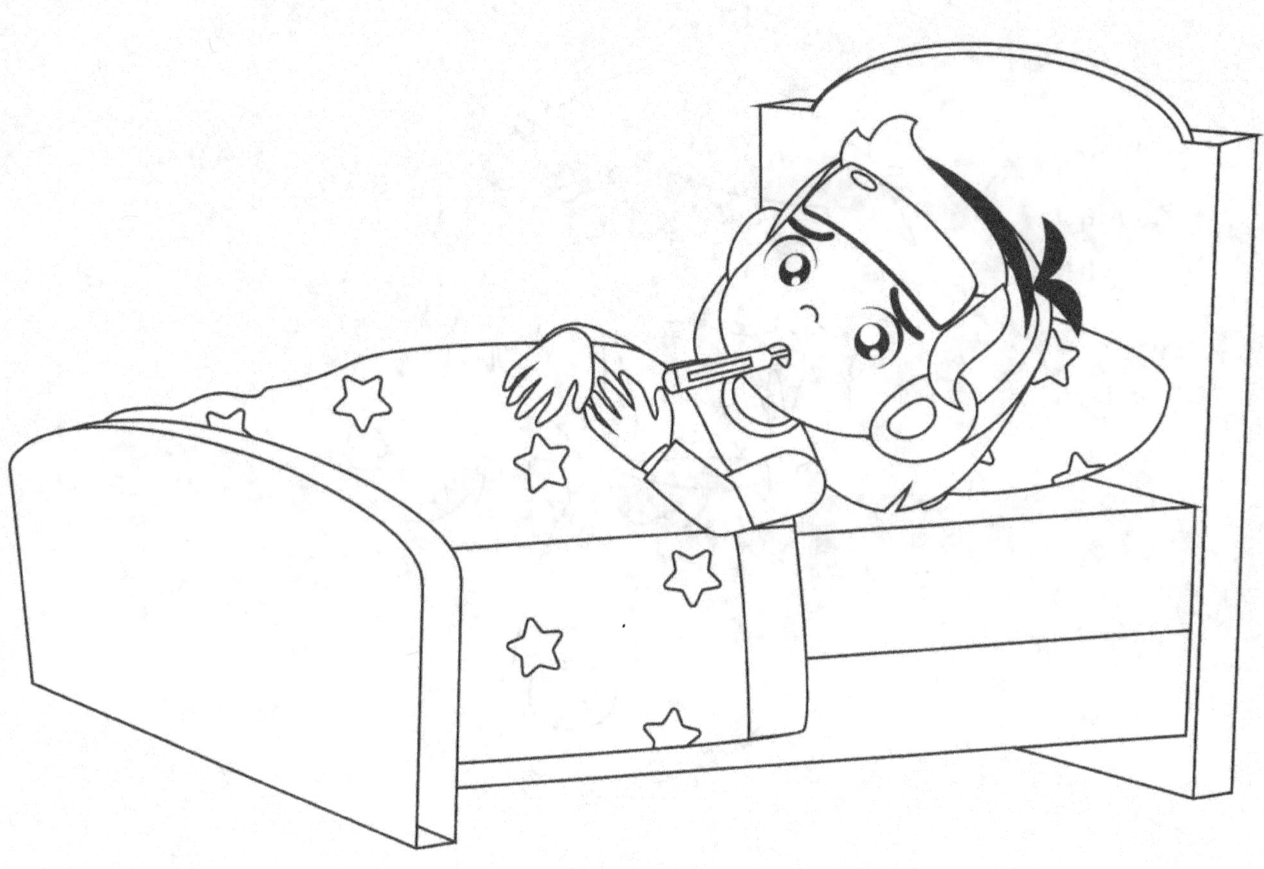

Cover your mouth and nose when you cough or sneeze

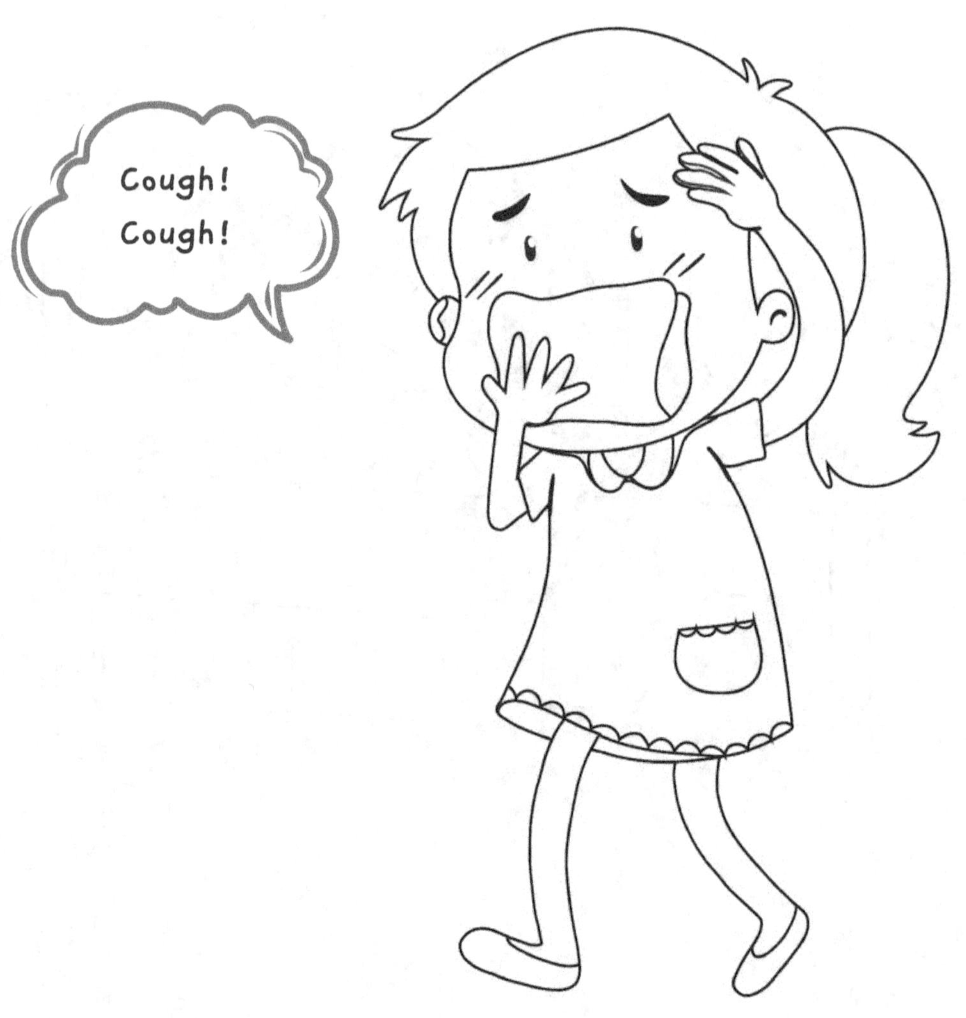

Keep these in mind every time you need to speak:

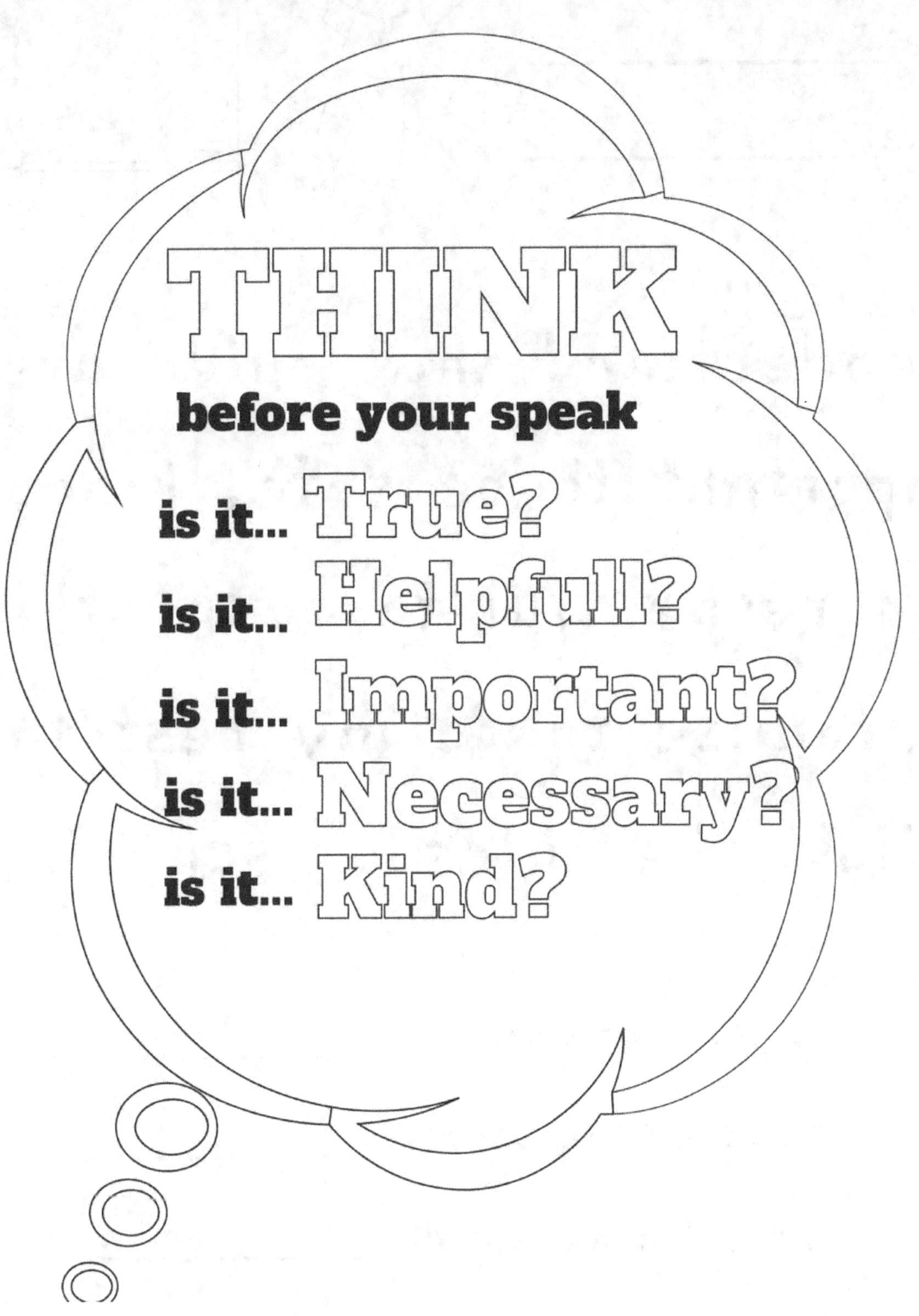

Class Rules Contract

Date:_______________

Name:_______________

I understand that rules are important to be safe, kind, and respectful to each other. I promise to do my best to follow the rules at school.

Child Signature: _____________

Teacher Signature: _____________

Parent Singnature: _____________

Congratulations!

You are an expert on the Class Rules!
Color your medal and cut it out to place it on the wall

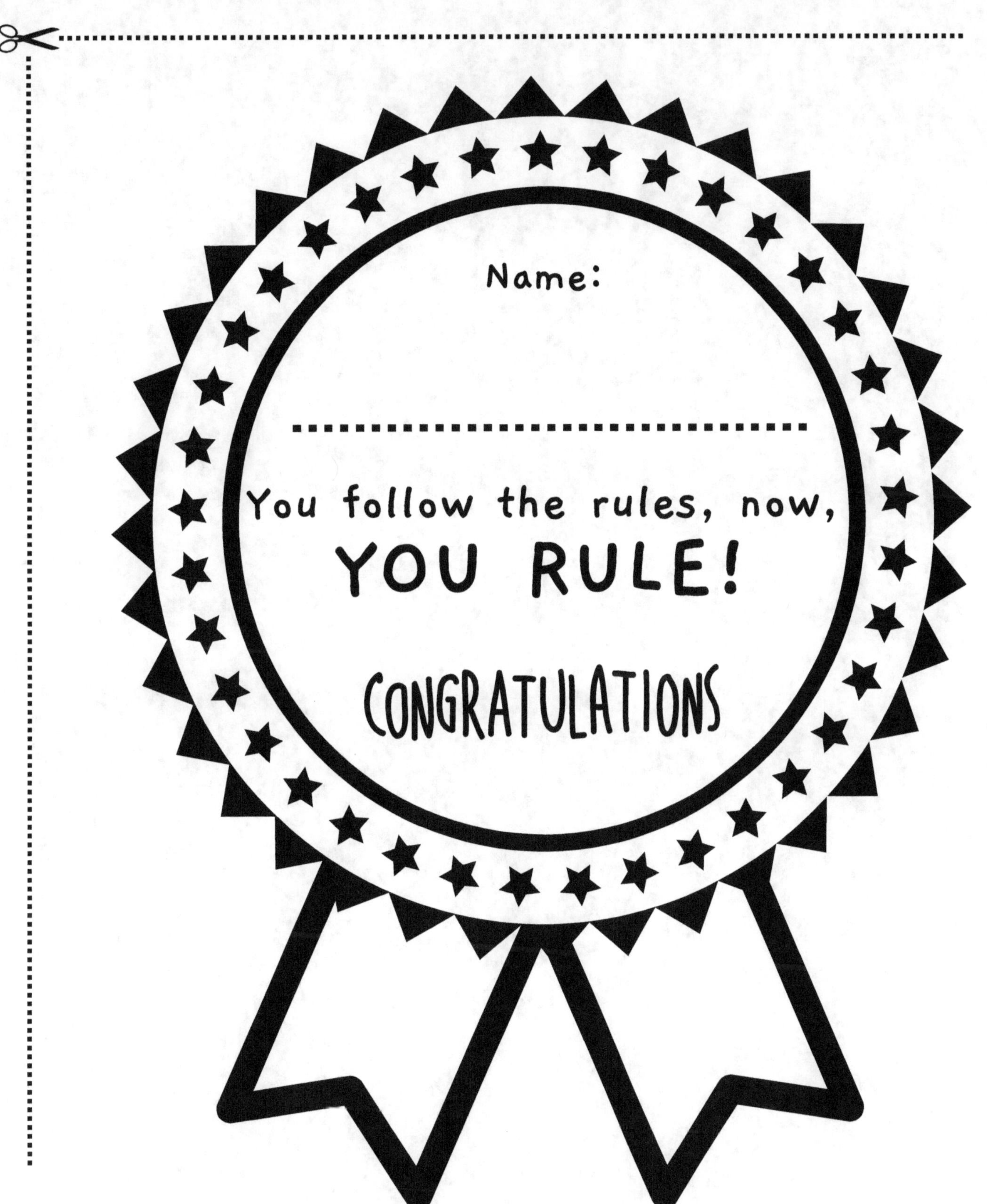

BACK TO SCHOOL